The children put on a play.

1

'I am the king,' said Chip.

2

'Fight the dragon.'

'I am the knight,' said Wilma.

'I will fight the dragon.'

'I am the dragon,' said Kipper.

6

'But I am a little dragon.'

'I am the princess,' said Biff.

'I like dragons.'

The princess played with the dragon.

10

They played under the tree.

'I am the knight,' said Wilma.

'I am frightened,' said the dragon.

'I am cross,' said the princess.

14

She pushed the knight in the pond.

'What a good play,' said everyone.

16

Contents

Introduction 5

🐾 Advice for Dog Walkers 6

Walk

1 Barrow Hills *(3 miles)*...8
2 Dyscarr Wood *(3 miles)* 12
3 Bevercotes Nature Reserve *(2½ or 4 miles)* 16
4 Harby & Doddington *(6 miles)* 20
5 Budby Forest & Hanger Hill Drive *(3 miles)* 25
6 The Teversal Trail *(4½ miles)*................................30
7 Oxclose Wood & Debdale *(2 miles)* 35
8 Ollerton Pit Wood *(3 miles)* 39
9 Vicar Water *(3 miles)* 43
10 Stapleford Wood *(4 miles)* 48
11 Edingley & the Southwell Trail *(2½ miles)* 52
12 Farndon Circular *(3 miles)* 56
13 Blidworth Wood *(3 miles)* 60
14 Brierley Forest Country Park *(3 miles)* 64
15 Moorgreen *(5 miles)* 68
16 Gunthorpe & the River Trent *(3½ miles)* 73
17 Bestwood Country Park *(4 miles)* 78
18 Cotgrave Forest *(4½ miles)* 82
19 Attenborough Wetlands *(2 miles)* 87
20 Ruddington & the Great Central Railway
      (4½ miles) 91

Appendix

🐾 Contact details for Small Animal Veterinary
   Practices in Nottinghamshire 96

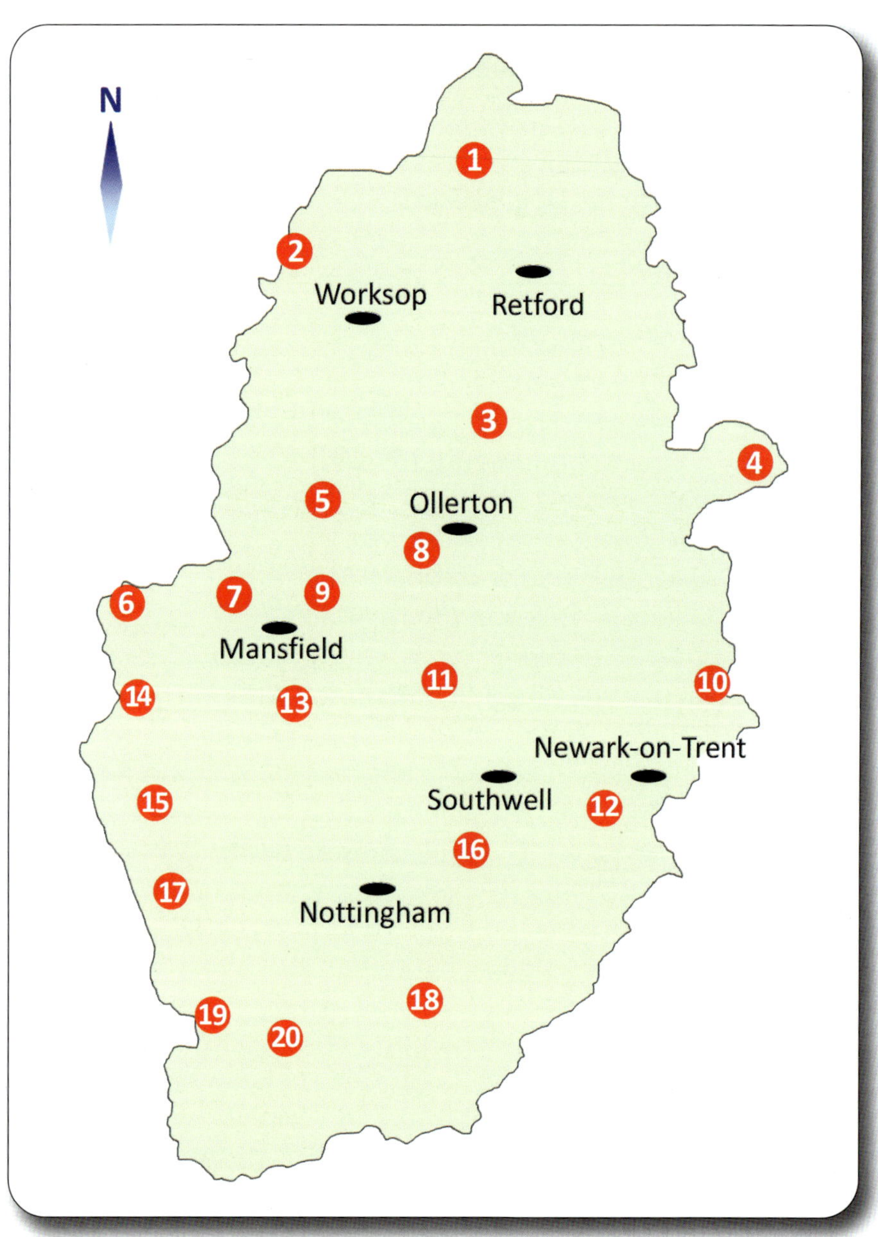

Area map showing location of the walks.

INTRODUCTION

This collection of walks is designed not only for caring dog owners, but for anyone interested in enjoying the countryside. In the process of preparing the book, I have explored many new routes in all parts of Nottinghamshire and met a variety of friendly owners and their dogs.

Through my job, in tourism, I have always promoted Nottinghamshire as a wonderful county for walking, with its interesting landscape including rivers, woodland, canals, heathland and reclaimed pit spoil heaps. Some of the circuits are on Forestry Commission land which are canine-friendly woods where dogs need to be on leads only in specific circumstances. In fact, dog walking is the most popular form of woodland recreation. The legacy of the coalfields in Nottinghamshire has given us some excellent brownfield walks, with outstanding views over the surrounding countryside.

I first walked the walks in this book with my two black Labradors, Macey and Jake. They were both friendly dogs and their idea of heaven was a good off-lead walk with other dogs, plenty of water and lots of sniffs. Sadly Jake passed away in 2013 and Macey in 2017. Thank you to 'Cassie' for accompanying me on the walks.

The walks in this book have been devised to ensure stiles and livestock are kept to a minimum. I have also tried to include routes where the dogs are able to run free.

I enjoy a good meal, home-made cake and excellent coffee so, where possible, I have included details of refreshment stops that welcome dogs.

My advice is to take your time and enjoy the wealth of sights, smells and wildlife that is out there for everyone. Have fun and remember – not only will your dog benefit from experiencing new environments but your own health will benefit too. Walking with a partner, either canine or human, can only add to the enjoyment.

Jane Broomhead

ADVICE FOR DOG WALKERS

'The countryside is a great place to exercise dogs, but it is every owner's duty to make sure their dog is not a danger or nuisance to farm animals, wildlife or other people.' (Taken from the Government's Code for the Public.) The full code is available on the Government's Countryside Access website: www.countrysideaccess.gov.uk The main points are:

- Keep dogs under proper control.
- Clean up after your dog.
- Go carefully on country roads.
- Fasten all gates.
- Keep to the paths across farmland.
- Protect plants and animals, and take your litter home.
- Consider other people. (Many of the paths used in this book are multi-purpose. Just one bad experience can make someone, especially children, frightened of dogs for life.) Look out for horse riders, cyclists and joggers. They can startle your dog and cause an injury or accident. It is always best to have third-party insurance for your dog.
- Be prepared. The countryside is a big adventure for your dog, but emergencies can arise when out for a walk. Heat stroke, insect stings, poisoning and adder bites are all potentially dangerous.

Some of the walks in this book are on nature reserves which are home to ground-nesting birds that need to be left undisturbed through the nesting season, from March to July. Around September is the time when pheasants are released for the shooting season. This is the case in some of the woodland walks, particularly Cotgrave Wood. Please observe any notices in such areas which typically advise that dogs should be kept on a lead.

Sheep and lambs will generally move away from dogs instinctively but unfortunately some dogs find that fun, and like to give chase which can cause ewes to abort. Lambing takes place from January to March. Livestock owners are entitled to shoot dogs worrying livestock.

Cattle are generally inquisitive and will move towards dogs, forming a semi-circle as they approach you. They are not usually harmful but a cow who considers her calf to be threatened may behave aggressively. If this should happen, do drop the lead and let your dog sort itself out. It is safer for both you and your dog.

Ticks

In my experience it is only during very hot weather that ticks can be found in Nottinghamshire. They tend to cling to the edge of scrub plants, particularly bracken. Both dogs and people can pick them up and their bite cannot be felt. You can reduce the chances by wearing long trousers, tucked into socks or boots, and long sleeves. Check yourself and your dog at the end of the walk and remove any ticks with tweezers or a special tick remover which can be bought. Ticks carry Lyme disease which can affect both people and dogs so prompt removal is important.

Seasonal Canine Illness

In Nottinghamshire there is also a problem with Seasonal Canine Illness. On-going tests have yet to confirm the cause of the illness. As a precaution, if your dog has any of the following symptoms after a walk, take them to a vet immediately:

- vomiting
- diarrhoea
- lethargy

. . . .

PUBLISHER'S NOTE

We hope that you obtain considerable enjoyment from this book; great care has been taken in its preparation. Although at the time of publication all routes followed public rights of way or permitted paths, diversion orders can be made and permissions withdrawn.

We cannot, of course, be held responsible for such diversion orders and any inaccuracies in the text which result from these or any other changes to the routes nor any damage which might result from walkers trespassing on private property. We are anxious though that all details covering the walks are kept up to date and would therefore welcome information from readers which would be relevant to future editions.

The simple sketch maps that accompany the walks in this book are based on notes made by the author whilst checking out the routes on the ground. They are designed to show you how to reach the start, to point out the main features of the overall circuit and they contain a progression of numbers that relate to the paragraphs of the text.

However, for the benefit of a proper map, we do recommend that you purchase the relevant Ordnance Survey sheet covering your walk. The Ordnance Survey maps are widely available, especially through booksellers and local newsagents.

Barrow Hills

Macey, ready to start the walk.

This is a quiet walk in the northern part of Nottinghamshire. The peace is occasionally marred by the planes from nearby Robin Hood airport but it is a lovely walk for dogs that enjoy their own company. The wood is an attractive Site of Special Scientific Interest (SSSI) and provides tantalising glimpses of panoramic views in all directions. The area to the north is very flat and was once known as the Vale of the Idle, a large proportion of which is only a few feet above sea level. The River Idle is formed 4 miles south of Retford at the confluence of the rivers Maun, Meden and Poulter.

During past times, the spring tides raised the level of the rivers Idle and Trent (into which the Idle flows) by five or six feet. This regular flooding of the land created swamps, but the silt deposited by the tidal water made very fertile soil. In the 17th century the celebrated local landowner and drainage engineer, Sir Cornelius Vermuyden, drained the land and built the Mother Dyke, a deep canal-like waterway which runs down the side of the Idle. There was also a succession of sluice gates which controlled the flood water. This area, to the north of the walk, is known today as the Carrs.

Terrain

There is one short steep descent on a woodland path. Theaker Lane, at the start of the walk, can be rutted and muddy.

Where to park

There is a large lay-by 1 mile from Bawtry on the A631, just after the start of the second section of dual-carriageway (GR: SK 666919). It is a short walk along the pavement to the start of the walk. **OS map:** Explorer 279 Doncaster.

How to get there

Take the A614 north from Nottingham. When the A614 reaches the A1 just north of Clumber Park join the A1 going north. After 4 miles leave the A1 following the signs for Bawtry A614. At the first traffic lights in Bawtry, turn right onto the A631 for Gainsborough. The walk begins 1 mile along this road.

Nearest refreshments

The **King William Inn**, Scaftworth. The small village of Scaftworth is on the opposite side of the dual-carriageway from the parking place. Here you will find the King William which is a dog friendly inn. The inn is open Monday to Thursday 5pm–9pm, Friday & Saturday 12 noon until 9pm and Sunday 12 noon until 7.45pm. ☎ 01302 710292. Postcode DN10 6BL. There are also several cafés in Bawtry with outside tables.

Dog factors

. . . .

Distance: 3 miles
Road walking: Some tracks are used by farm traffic. A short section is on a quiet road in Harwell village.
Livestock: None
Stiles: None
Nearest vets: Raoul Dowding, Bawtry. ☎ 01302 711922.

The Walk

1 Walk east along the pavement, away from Bawtry, for about 50 yards until a green lane is reached. There is a 'Byways' signpost pointing to the left. This is **Theaker Lane**. Follow this unmade track until it becomes grassy and rutted. Continue straight on with **Barrow Hills Wood** across the field on the right.

2 After passing a small wood on the right, next to the track, the path widens and becomes a farm lane. Keep straight on (beware of farm traffic) until **Harwell** village is reached. Turn right, up the village street.

The village of Harwell has an interesting name, which is thought to be derived from the old English 'here' and 'wella' or 'the army springs'. The village is close to the Roman road which ran from the River Trent at Littleborough in Nottinghamshire to Doncaster in South Yorkshire. This was more than likely marked as a place for clean and reliable water.

3 On reaching Pinfold Lane, with a Public Footpath sign and a brown wooden board reading '**Public Footpath to Barrow Hills**', turn right. Walk up the unmade road past the houses until a wooden gate is reached at the top on the right. Go round the small gate and enter the wood.

Barrow Hills Wood is unusual in that it constitutes glacial sand and calcareous clay nodules, more associated with coastal areas and Breckland, than northern Nottinghamshire. Due to this there is a wide range of flora, including vipers bugloss, basil, thyme and musk. The resident bird population includes tree creeper, green

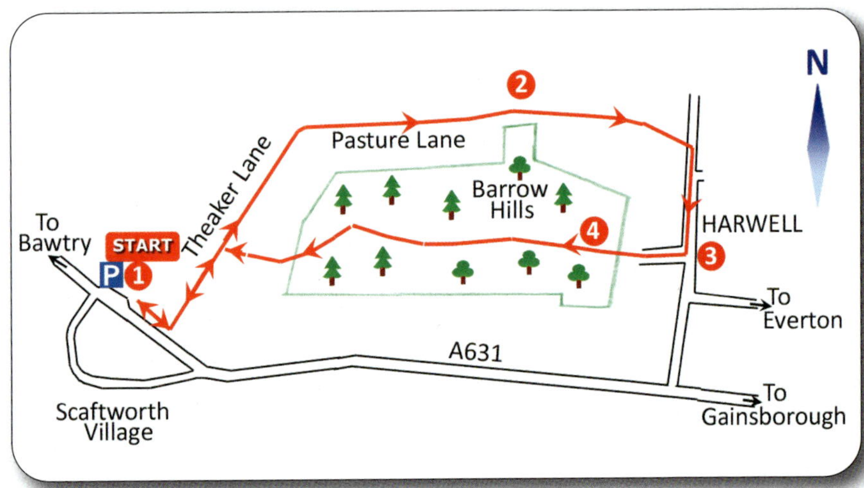

About to enter the woods.

woodpecker, lesser spotted woodpecker, long-tailed tit and sparrow hawk. The wood is managed by Everton Village Council.

4 The path is fairly wide and continues straight through the wood. Eventually, a large yew tree is reached, here the wider path bends to the left. Continue straight on with the yew tree on your left. Towards the edge of the wood, keep straight on steeply downhill to join another path. Turn left with a yellow topped footpath sign post on your left. Take the next right with a yellow topped footpath sign on the right and follow the narrow path with hedges and fields on either side to reach **Theaker Lane**. Turn left and follow the track back to the main road. Turn right on reaching the main road to return to the car park.

2

Dyscarr Wood

We're waiting for you!

This is a lovely walk on mostly level paths, exceptional in early spring when the wood is carpeted with wood anemones, common dog violet and lesser celandines. These are followed by sweet woodruff, primroses and then ramsons, with their smell of garlic. The route begins at Langold Country Park and continues through Dyscarr Wood, a semi-natural elm and ash wood with some areas of scrub and marsh. It is part-owned and managed by Nottinghamshire Wildlife Trust.

The walk then crosses into South Yorkshire down a well-trodden path along the sides of arable farmland with far reaching views. Summer visitors include the blackcap and whitethroat; skylarks can be heard over the open fields in spring.

Langold Country Park, at the start of the walk, was originally designed as a formal estate by Sir Geoffrey Wyatt in the early 1800s. It was intended that the estate's hall should overlook the lake from its northern bank. Although the foundations for the hall were laid in 1818, the project was abandoned. The 400-acre park is now run by Bassetlaw District Council and is mostly used for fishing and walking. Around the park there are at least seven known species of bats. Bats are long-lived, intelligent, highly mobile and more agile in flight than most birds.

Terrain

Woodland paths and field verges which can be muddy after rain. The walk is mostly on level ground.

Where to park

Park at the small car park for Langold Country Park just off the A60 (GR: SK 585866). There is also a larger car park near Langold Lake. **OS map:** Explorer 279 Doncaster.

How to get there

From the A60, 7 miles north of Worksop just before Langold village, you will find the car park on the left in a dip just before the sign for Langold. Alternatively, continue to the top of the hill and turn left and left again into Church Street. Continue to the end of the road following the brown information signs for Langold Country Park and begin the walk from point 2.

Nearest refreshments

Andy's Park Café is situated next to the car park. It is open daily and serves anything from ice cream to bacon rolls. Although dogs are not allowed in the café, there is outside seating. Postcode S81 9NW. ☎ 07740 462593.

Dog factors

Distance: 3 miles
Road walking: A very small section on a quiet road in Langold Country Park.
Livestock: None
Stiles: None
Nearest vets: Wildbore Veterinary Ltd, Worksop. ☎ 01909 472059.

The Walk

- -

1 From the car park, walk across the undulating green, keeping slightly to the right to reach a path through the trees which runs close to the houses on the north side of the park boundary. After 300 yards the path emerges to meet the road to **Langold Lake**. The lake is just visible on the left behind the new large outdoor children's play area.

The lake is worth a short detour as it was here that the British Long-Distance Swimming Association Championships were traditionally held. The Langold Gala, centred on the lake, was first held in 1929 and attracted over 10,000 people in its heyday. A regular highlight of the gala in the 1970s was the fire dive performed by the Langold Lake Manager, Jack Revill, from the lake's 30-ft-high diving board. The board was removed in 1983. Although the lido has now been drained, it is still possible to see the remains on the south side of the lake.

2 At the road turn right and walk up to the park entrance. Turn left and go round the barrier and take the right-hand gravel path through **Dyscarr Wood**. There is an information board on the right. Follow this path for about ¾ mile

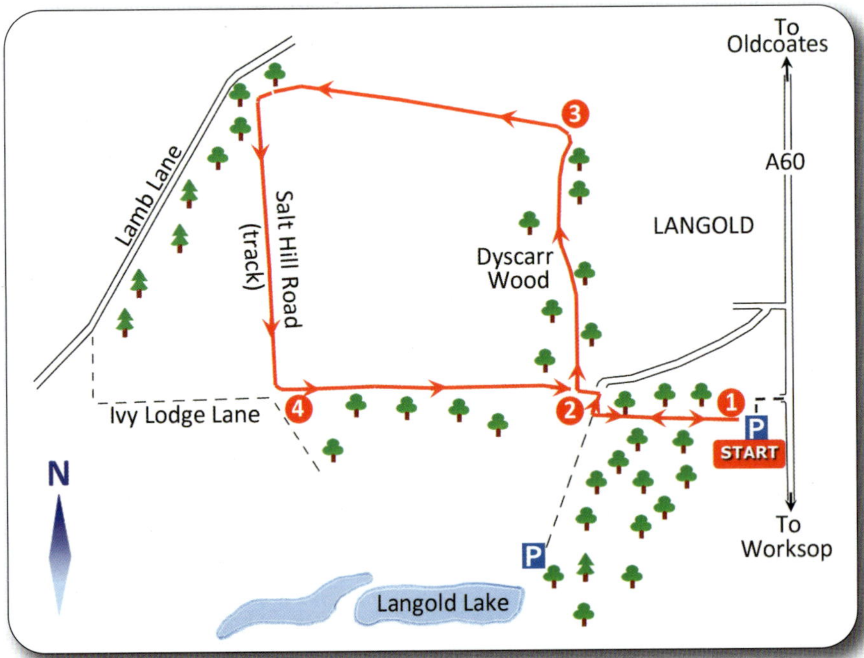

through the wood keeping right at the stone post with '**Rowbothams Round Rotherham**' on the post.

3 Immediately on leaving the wood, turn left with a yellow topped Footpath sign on your right. Follow the wide track along the field verge, with a hedge on your left. Eventually you reach a small wood (please be aware that there is a busy road ahead). After entering the wood take the narrow path on the left which runs down the field side of the wood. When the path joins a wider path, turn left towards a field, there is a small wooden post on the left with a yellow arrow and a Doorstep Walk sign. Follow this track along the edge of the field for about ¾ mile to reach a green barrier before a road.

The three fields on the left make up what was known as the oval, now known locally as the racecourse. Anthony St Leger lived nearby at Firbeck from 1763 to 1780. In 1776 it was reputed that a race was held between his horse and another round the oval, a distance of about 9 furlongs, and this was believed to be the first running of the world's oldest classic race, the St Leger, now held annually at Doncaster.

4 The track bends left just before the green barrier and continues down a well-defined bridleway with an open field on the left. The path eventually re-enters Dyscarr Wood, continue straight on until the entrance barrier is reached. At the barrier, turn right into **Langold Country Park**, then turn left retracing your steps to the car park.

The woods in springtime.

Bevercotes Nature Reserve

The bridge over the River Meden.

This walk is Labrador heaven, or at least I'm sure that's what Jake and Macey think, as most of the paths have drainage ditches at the side which are excellent for paddling in on a hot summer day.

If you are an avid entomologist, birdwatcher or just generally interested in all forms of wildlife, this is definitely the walk for you. The drone of the traffic on the nearby A1 fades into the background as you watch the antics of the common blue damselflies around the small lake or black-tailed skimmers darting along the River Meden. Birdwatchers are not forgotten, with many species on the site, including the kingfisher. In December 2009 a Siberian stonechat was photographed.

I have spent many hours here searching for dingy skipper butterflies, not finding any until recently. Instead I found lots of Mother Shipton moths which are common here in early June, so-called because of the outline of Mother Shipton's face on their wings.

The site has been managed by the Forestry Commission with help from Nottinghamshire County Council since 2006 and consists of conifer and mixed woodland plantations, two small lakes, ponds and two minor rivers.

Terrain

Well-maintained wide stony paths. There are two gentle climbs. In wet weather there can be a lot of standing water at the sides of the paths. A concrete bridge joins both sides of the site, with a fast-flowing river which has steep banks. There are also several ponds and two small lakes.

Where to park

Park in the lay-by on the unmarked minor road (GR SK 696735). **OS map:** Explorer 270 Sherwood Forest, and Explorer 271 Newark/Retford. The walk starts on map 270.

How to get there

From the A614 Nottingham to Doncaster road, continue north from the Ollerton roundabout. At the next roundabout (Thoresby) turn right, signed to Bothamsall. Follow the road through Bothamsall to the T-junction and turn left signed for Retford onto the B6387. Towards the end of the long straight, turn right onto an unmarked minor road with a blue Route 6 Cycle Trail sign to Harby & Lincoln. This is part of the Dukeries Cycle Trail. Continue over the bridges spanning the old Bevercotes colliery workings, round a sharp right-hand bend and park in the second lay-by on the left. The entrance to the nature reserve is at the end of the lay-by.

Nearest refreshments

What is nicer on a hot summer's day than a delicious home-made ice cream? Return over the former colliery bridges to the main road and turn right. After 200 yards turn left for **Thaymar Ice Cream**. This ice cream parlour and café has outside tables on the veranda, and you can try over 30 mouth-watering flavours of ice cream. The café which uses local produce is open seven days a week from 10 am to 5 pm. Postcode DN22 8DB. ☎ 01623 862632.

Dog factors

Distance: 4 miles (This can easily be shortened to 2½ miles for less active dogs).
Road walking: None
Livestock: None
Stiles: None
Nearest vets: Portland House Veterinary Group, Retford. ☎ 01777 703663.

The Walk

1 From the entrance barrier walk towards the large information boards. Turn right and follow the wide path which bends to the left and continues down a long straight for ¾ mile. There is a pond on the right halfway down the straight. Continue round a long sweeping left-hand bend with a small lake on the right. Pass a small private wood on the right and reach a crossroads.

The wide grassy verges are home to a diversity of butterflies and day-flying moths, including common blue, large and small skipper butterflies, and five-spot burnet and shaded broad bar moths,

2 Turn left at the crossroads going steeply uphill following the path round a right-hand bend to reach a T-junction. Turn right down the hill to reach a concrete bridge. There is a small lake on the left. If you wish to take the shorter route, turn left just before the lake. For the full route, cross the bridge over the **River Meden**.

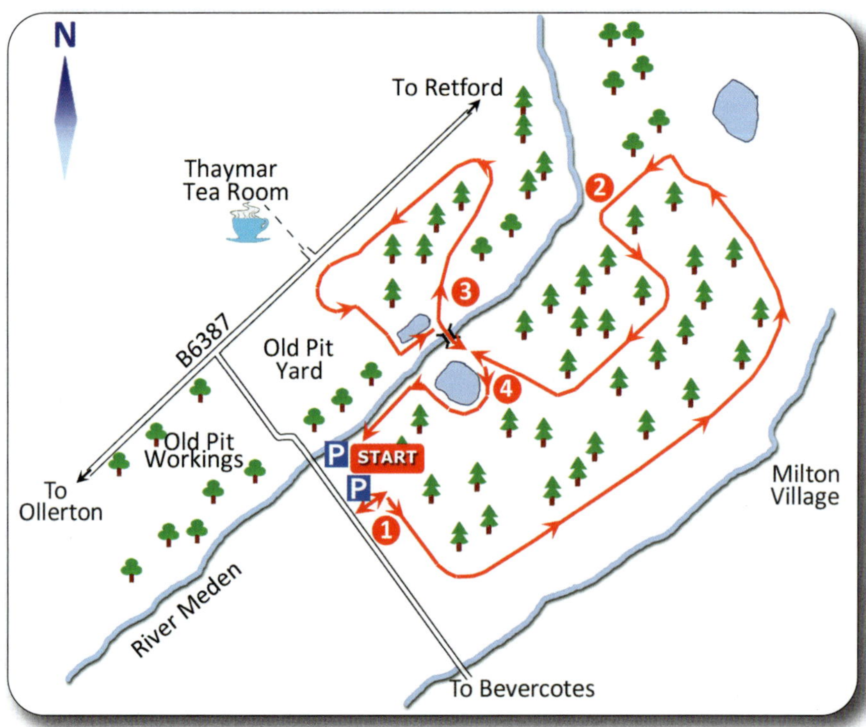

Take time to check for kingfishers and the abundant dragonflies, damselflies and skimmers. The River Meden joins with the Maun on the east side of the reserve and, together with the Poulter, they form the River Idle just north of the A1. The Idle meanders northwards through Retford and joins the Trent at West Stockwith. North of Retford is a wide flood plain which forms a wetland habitat for many bird species. The Nottinghamshire Wildlife Trust's Idle Valley Centre is an excellent place to watch wading birds.

③ Keep to the right up the slope, following a wide path round a left-hand bend. On reaching a Y-junction take the right-hand path going slowly downhill towards the former concreted **Bevercotes Pit Yard**.

When it opened in 1963 Bevercotes was hailed as a '21st-century colliery' and was one of the deepest mines in Britain. It closed in 1993.

Follow the path rejoining the main trail, turn right and follow the wider path downhill. The path now bends to the left round a pond and then turns right, back over the concrete bridge.

④ Carry straight on with the lake on your right, the track bends to the right, round the water, it then curves to the left back to the road. Watch out for some very dirty drainage ditches on the left-hand side before the information boards.

Looking down the long straight to Milton.

Harby & Doddington

Near the old railway bridge.

This long walk for active dogs is full of history and is suitable for a lovely spring day or summer picnic. Sometimes it's wonderful to have a long quiet stroll with your 'best friend'; dogs enjoy the occasional full day out followed by contented sleep. This route is too far for my older less active dog, but Macey loves a long walk.

Although the walk starts in Nottinghamshire, it soon crosses the boundary into Lincolnshire using a disused railway line. Then it passes close to Doddington Hall. My first introduction to this wonderful hall was when we did a sponsored dog walk, which still happens every year in the spring.

The walk continues on to Harby, the village where Eleanor, Queen to Edward I, died in 1290. Edward and Eleanor had left Westminster in July for a northern tour around Northamptonshire and Nottinghamshire, staying lastly at the Royal Hunting Lodge at Clipstone. When the queen fell ill they left Clipstone for Lincoln, but were forced to lodge with Richard de Weston at the Harby Manor House as her condition worsened. Here she died and her body was taken to Lincoln to be embalmed, while her viscera were buried in a marble tomb within Lincoln Cathedral.

Edward was distraught, as theirs had been a very happy marriage. 'Eleanor' crosses were erected at each of the nightly stopping places on his return journey to Westminster, the first being erected in Lincoln and the last at Charing Cross. Only three of the original crosses remain in place, at Geddington, Hardingstone and Waltham.

Terrain

Disused railway track, now with a new tarmac surface, grassy tracks and gravel farm roads. The walk is nearly all on the level.

Where to park

There is limited parking in Harby village, or on the road just before the railway bridge (GR: SK 881714) near the access to the unused railway line (please do not park in the fields). It is possible to start the walk at point 3 at the church next to Doddington Hall where there is overspill parking. **OS maps:** Explorer 271 Newark-on-Trent/Retford, and Explorer 272 Lincoln.

How to get there

From the Markham Moor junction on the A1 take the A57 towards Lincoln crossing the River Trent at Dunham on Trent (this is a toll bridge, currently 30p per car). After crossing the river, take the next right signed to Newark A1133. After 2 miles turn left down Moor Lane signed to Thorney and Wigsley. At the first crossroads turn right into Wigsley village. At the T-junction turn left signed for Harby. There is limited parking around the village hall, or turn left on Low Street (signed for Lincoln) and after the school there is parking on the left just before the railway bridge.

Dog factors

Distance: 6 miles
Road walking: A small section in Doddington village and about ½ mile in Harby. There is one busy road to cross in Doddington.
Livestock: None
Stiles: None
Nearest vets: Southwell Minster Veterinary Centre, Newark.
☎ 01636 612906.

Nottinghamshire – A Dog Walker's Guide

From Newark-on-Trent, turn left off the A46 (Lincoln Road) onto the A1133 through Collingham. Continue to Besthorpe taking a right turn just after the village. Continue straight on this road until Harby is reached.

Nearest refreshments

There is an award-winning farm shop and café next to Doddington Hall which is about two-thirds round the walk. Dogs are welcome at the outside tables. This very popular café is open from 10 am to 5 pm and can get very busy. Postcode LN6 4RT. ☎ 01522 688581.

The Walk

1 If parking in Harby, walk down **Low Street** past the school to reach the railway bridge. Take the walkway on the left of the bridge which will take you onto the disused railway track. Turn right and go under the bridge following the track for about 1½ miles.

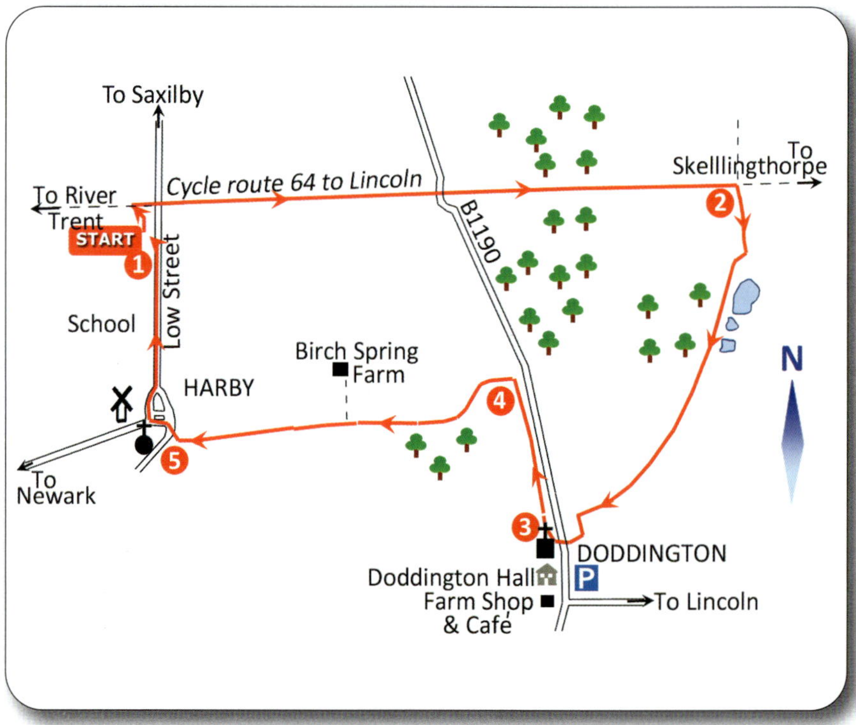

2 At a well-defined crossroads, with a restricted byway signpost, turn right by a wooden gate. On reaching another signpost just after a red 'no fishing' sign turn right down a public bridleway. Please place dogs on leads as there are deep ponds on the left. Follow the track keeping the ponds on your left and an attractive wood on your right. (**Ash Lound**). The track continues as a field verge to **Doddington**. Carry on past the houses to reach a main road.

The village of Doddington is mentioned in the Domesday Book and was probably founded in Saxon times. Although dogs are not allowed in the hall or gardens, Doddington Hall built in 1585 by Robert Smythson is well worth a visit. The gardens are now fully restored and produce a variety of vegetables for the café and farm shop. There is a varied programme of workshops and events throughout the year, details of which are available on their web site.

St Peter's church, Doddington.

3 Cross the road with care and follow the public bridleway to the right of the church. Continue down the bridleway which is separated from the busy main road by a hedge.

4 Turn left at the track for **Birch Spring Farm**, following the gravel drive for about ½ mile. The bridleway continues straight ahead at the driveway to the farm onto a grassy track. Please respect the notice which politely asks for dogs to be on a lead. The path then crosses an arable field (the field was being ploughed when I did this walk so we walked round the verge). You are heading for a gap in the hedge with an open wooden gate. Continue straight on, with a muddy ditch on your left, heading towards **Harby** and a large green barn.

5 On approaching **Harby** the track narrows with a smallholding on your right. Turn right at the children's play area to reach a village road. At the give way sign turn left and then right onto **Low Street**. Either return to your car in the village or continue down **Low Street** past the school to your car.

Budby Forest & Hanger Hill Drive

In the forest.

This **mostly level walk** takes in the far side of Sherwood Forest and can easily be extended to include Budby Common Nature Reserve. For those wanting an even longer walk for more active dogs, it can be extended to the Sherwood Forest Visitor Centre or Clumber Park. If you continue south passing the first signpost and take the next right track opposite the Sherwood Forest Visitor Centre boundary, then just before joining Hanger Hill Drive, is the recently discovered Thynhowe, on Hanger Hill. The site has yet to reveal all of its many mysteries but it is thought to have been a meeting place for over 1,000 years and could have marked the boundary between the kingdoms of Northumbria and Mercia.

Known as Birklands, this part of Sherwood Forest passed from the Crown into the estates of the Dukeries in 1818. Hanger Hill Drive is thought to have been constructed to provide access to the pleasure grounds of Birklands from

Nottinghamshire – A Dog Walker's Guide

Welbeck Abbey. It was also known as Lady Anne's Drive and may well have been created for a visit by Queen Anne around 300 years ago.

During the 19th and 20th centuries the commercial forest was expanded, with new conifer plantations covering much of the heathland. Although there is evidence of felling along the walk, the area is still heavily forested.

Terrain

Wide, well-maintained tracks, mostly on the level. There are two crossings of a busy road with restricted views. A very small section on the verge of a busy road. Some of the walk is on the very popular Cycle Route 6 which runs from Clumber Park to Sherwood Pines.

Where to park

Park at the end of the no through lane where there is ample space by the railings (GR: SK 604702). **OS map:** Explorer 270 Sherwood Forest.

How to get there

On the A614 north of Nottingham, reach the Ollerton roundabout and take the A616 for Sheffield/Worksop. After going through Budby turn left at a mini roundabout onto the A616 to Sheffield. Very soon turn left onto Netherfield Lane signed for Meden Vale and Warsop. At the end of the long straight, 100 yards after the National Cycle Route signs, turn left onto the cycle route. There is a sign for ST (Severn-Trent Water Ltd) Budby on the right. Continue past the Water Station and park at the end of the road by the railings.

Nearest refreshments

The **Old School Tea Room** at Carburton where many dog walkers use the outside decking to sample the delicious lunches and cakes. The tea room is open from 10 am to 4 pm (closed Mondays). Turn right onto Netherfield Lane and then right again to reach the mini roundabout at Budby. Turn left onto the Worksop road, follow this for about 1½ miles, the tea room is on the left at the Carburton crossroads. Postcode S80 3BP. ☎ 01909 483517.

Dog factors

Distance: 3 miles
Road walking: 20 yards on the grass verge of a busy road.
Livestock: None
Stiles: None
Nearest vets: Portland House Veterinary Group, New Ollerton, Newark. ☎ 01623 860138.

The Walk

1 Walk south round the green barrier onto a wide track. There is a blue National Cycle Route 6 sign. Continue down the long straight to reach a crossroads. Turn right following the public bridleway sign for Warsop. (If you wish to continue to see Budby Common or the Sherwood Forest Visitor Centre continue straight on here). This wide track eventually goes downhill to reach another crossroads.

2 Turn right onto **Hanger Hill Drive**. Follow the road slightly downhill. At the edge of the forest make sure dogs are on leads as there is a busy road ahead.

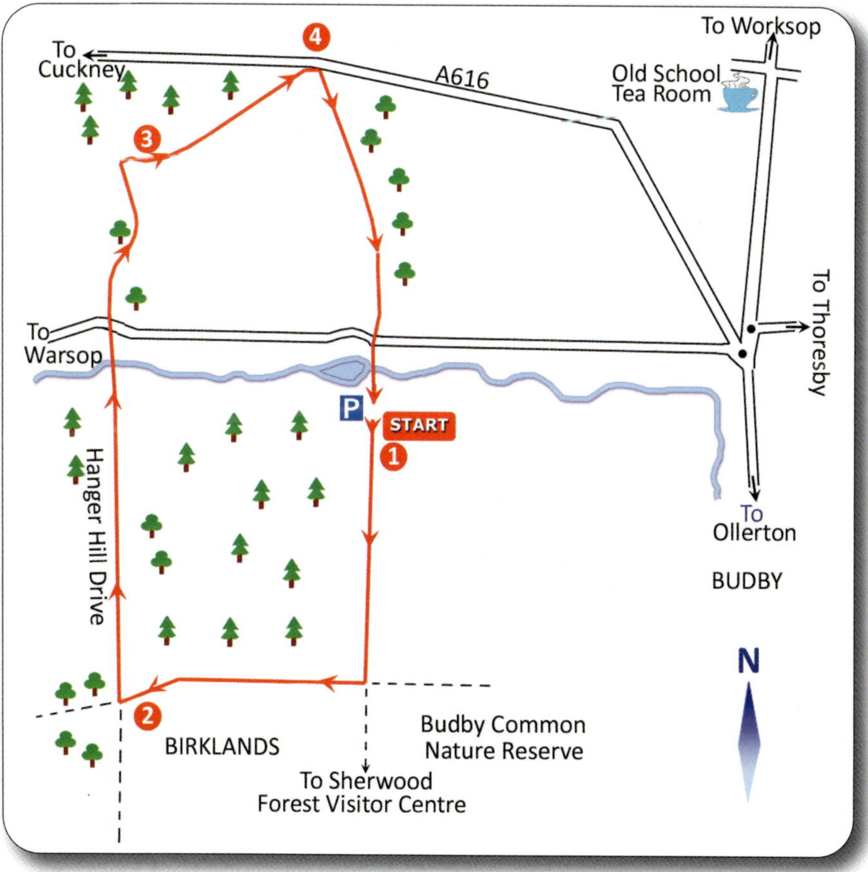

Macey, checking out the verge.

The culvert that carries water beneath the drive is part of the water meadows scheme created by the 4th Duke of Portland, check out the quality of the stonework. To the left of the circular earthwork is a Second World War machine-gun post.

On reaching the road, cross with care onto a narrow woodland path. Continue through the trees to reach a crossroads.

3 At the crossroads turn right following a public footpath sign, this has woodland on the left and a large field on the right. Before reaching the top of the field and no later than passing a metal gate in the hedge, please place dogs on leads as a major road is ahead.

4 On reaching the road, turn right down the road verge for 20 yards and then turn right by a multi-user path sign and a concessionary bridleway sign. (If you wish to carry on to Clumber Park, then cross the road and follow the Route 6 Cycleway). This pleasant path meanders downhill. At the second seat on the right please place dogs on leads again as there is a busy road ahead. Cross the road with care and continue straight ahead back to your car.

The Teversal Trail

At the visitor centre.

This is a walk the dogs and I have long enjoyed, seeing the improvements to the trail which have been made over the years, especially at the Derbyshire end. For the purpose of this walk I have used the Teversal Visitor Centre as the starting point which is in Nottinghamshire. I sometimes use the car park at the Pleasley Pit Country Park in Derbyshire from where you can reach the trail from the north. If you wish to use this car park, it is on Pit Lane in Pleasley village.

The Teversal Visitor Centre, which opened in 1993, is very dog-friendly. There are exhibitions and reference books on the local area should you wish to find further information. There is an abundance of picnic tables outside.

The walk is nearly all on disused railway track beds and almost forms a complete triangle. As the last railway section was closed in 1978, nature has had many years to colonise the site with an abundance of wild flowers, butterflies and birds in the various habitats along the trail. Please be aware there are cuttings and embankments with very steep sides on the old railway line. In some sections I am unable to throw the ball for Macey for fear of them both going over the side.

Terrain

The trail is flat with an even surface but in some sections there are steep drops on either side of the path. Halfway round there is a short section of track used by farm vehicles.

Where to park

There is a large free car park at the Teversal Visitor Centre, Carnarvon Street, Frackley Road, NG17 3HJ (GR: SK 479614) **OS map:** Explorer 269 Chesterfield.

How to get there

From Mansfield follow the B6014 through Skegby to a roundabout. Turn right down Frackley Road. Follow the brown sign for the Teversal Visitor Centre, turning right down Carnarvon Street. The car park is at the bottom of the road. If using the northern entrance at Pleasley Pit, use the car park (SK500644) and walk south past the large pond and join the trail after crossing the farm track (just after point 3).

Nearest refreshments

The visitor centre café opens at 10.30 am every day except Monday. No hot food is served after 2 pm. Postcode NG17 3HJ ☎ 01623 442021.

Dog factors

Distance: 4½ miles
Road walking: None, but there are two crossings of minor roads.
Livestock: None, but the trail is used by horse riders.
Stiles: None
Nearest vets: Thompsons Veterinary Surgery, Sutton-in-Ashfield. ☎ 01623 555460.

The Walk

. . . .

1 From the car park walk north from the visitor centre past the coal garden and go through the gate onto the trail. Turn right, signed **Skegby** 1¼ miles, following the trail for about 1 mile to reach a triangular junction. Turn left.

This next section of track was part of the Midland Railway Westhouses to Mansfield Woodhouse branch which opened as a complete route in 1886 and closed to passenger traffic in 1930.

Approaching point 3 of the walk.

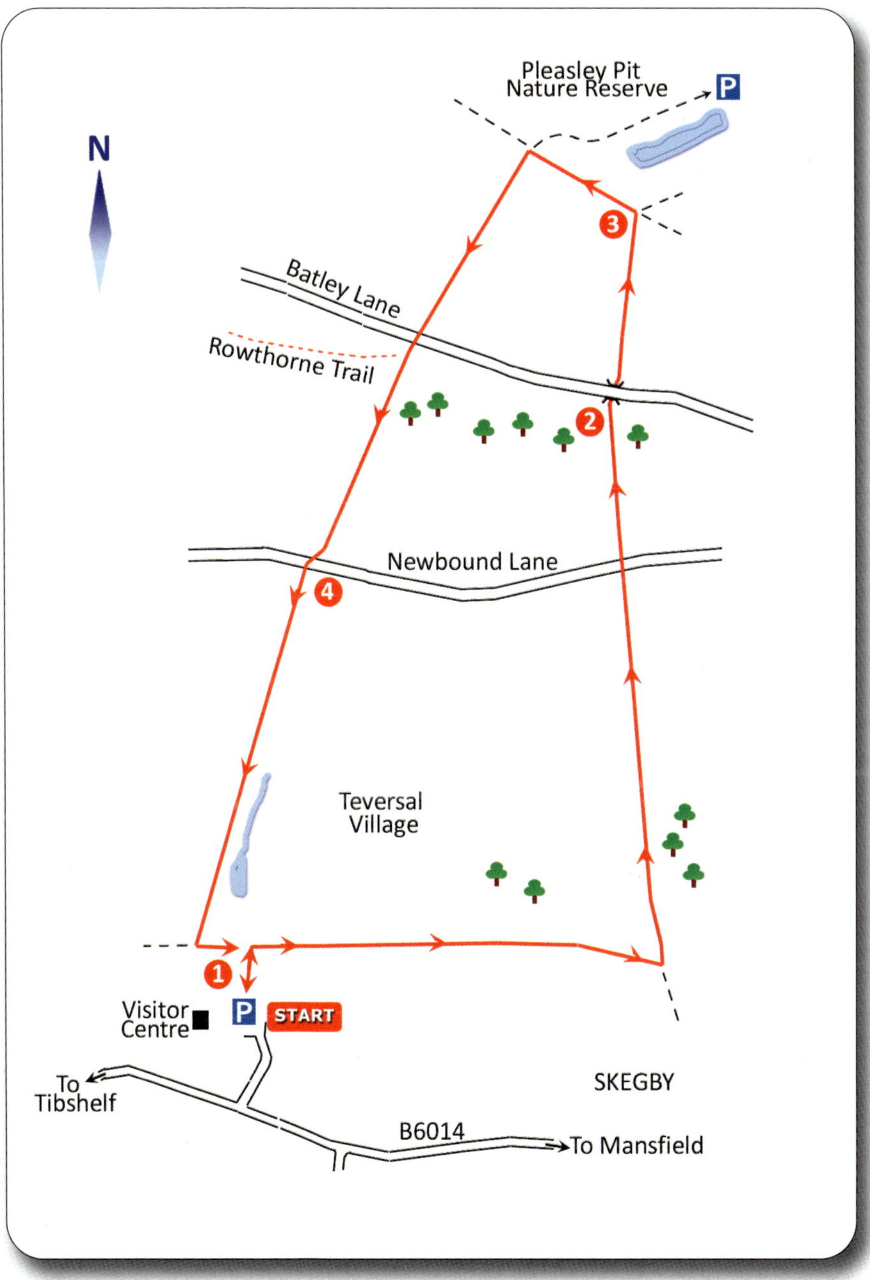
N
Pleasley Pit
Nature Reserve
P
3
Batley Lane
Rowthorne Trail
2
Newbound Lane
4
Teversal
Village
1
Visitor
Centre
P
START
To
Tibshelf
SKEGBY
B6014
To Mansfield

2 Continue along the track for a further ¼ mile. Just after passing the Derbyshire sign there is a minor road crossing. Go down the steps, cross the road and continue straight ahead. This next section is known as the mini '**Creswell Craggs**'. Walk up the trail to reach a junction.

3 Turn left following the farm road for about 200 yards. At a crossroads turn left signed for the **Teversal Trail**. **Pleasley Pit Park** is on the right. Follow this track for about ¼ mile.

You will pass the signs for the Rowthorne Trail, a disused railway line which was known as the Doe Lea branch and ran from Staveley to Pleasley. It was never well patronised and closed in July 1930.

4 At the end of the long straight the path rises and a minor road is crossed by going right, over the bridge and then turning left, back onto the trail. After a further mile, the track widens and reaches a large junction. Turn left and then directly right back to the visitor centre car park.

Oxclose Wood & Debdale

One of the two viewpoint 'walls' passed on the route.

Situated in the urban area of Mansfield Woodhouse, this surprisingly quiet, completely off-road walk, has superb views. There is even a large pond for those hot days when nothing but a cooling paddle will do.

This brownfield walk uses the old spoil heaps of Sherwood Colliery which have been planted with silver birch and conifers to form Oxclose Wood. There are some magnificent views from the top overlooking Mansfield and the surrounding countryside. There are two viewpoint 'walls', both constructed of Bulwell/Linby stone (magnesian limestone) which is used extensively in the local area.

The Ellis family from Hucknall sank Sherwood Colliery in 1902. Two shafts were sunk between 1902 and 1903. By 1934 Sherwood had pit head baths and by 1983 both winders were electrified. Production ceased in 1992. The site is managed by Nottinghamshire County Council and the Forestry Commission.

Terrain

Mostly level walking on well-maintained stony paths. There is a long steep ascent to the top of the old spoil heap and two short descents. There is a large pond close to the start.

Where to park

Free parking at Mansfield Woodhouse station (GR: SK 534632). **OS map:** Explorer 270 Sherwood Forest.

How to get there

From the A60 north of Mansfield turn left onto the A6075 signed to Sutton-in-Ashfield. Follow the road under the railway bridge and take the next turning right (The Sidings) signed for Mansfield Woodhouse station. From the A619 Mansfield to Chesterfield road take the A6075 signed for Mansfield Woodhouse and then follow the signs for Mansfield Woodhouse station. Follow the road under the barrier (height restriction) into the station car park. Please park as near as possible to the bottom left-hand corner.

Dog factors

Distance: 2 miles
Road walking: None
Livestock: None
Stiles: None
Nearest vets: Park Hall Veterinary Clinic, Mansfield Woodhouse.
☎ 01623 620784.

Nearest refreshments

How about a good fish and chip shop? Why not try **Seaqueen Fisheries**? This popular takeaway is open between 11.30 am to 2 pm and then again at 4.30 pm until 10 pm. It is closed on Sundays. They have an extensive menu with lots of 'extras'. From the car park turn left under the bridge and go straight across the traffic lights. Turn left at the next junction and then directly right, passing Morrisons supermarket on the left. Go straight across the next traffic lights and the Fisheries is on the left (2 miles). Postcode NG19 9LE. ☎ 01623 627406.

The Walk

. . . .

1 Climb the steps at the bottom left-hand side of the car park. Carry straight on past the large noticeboards to a junction. Go straight across, keeping on the

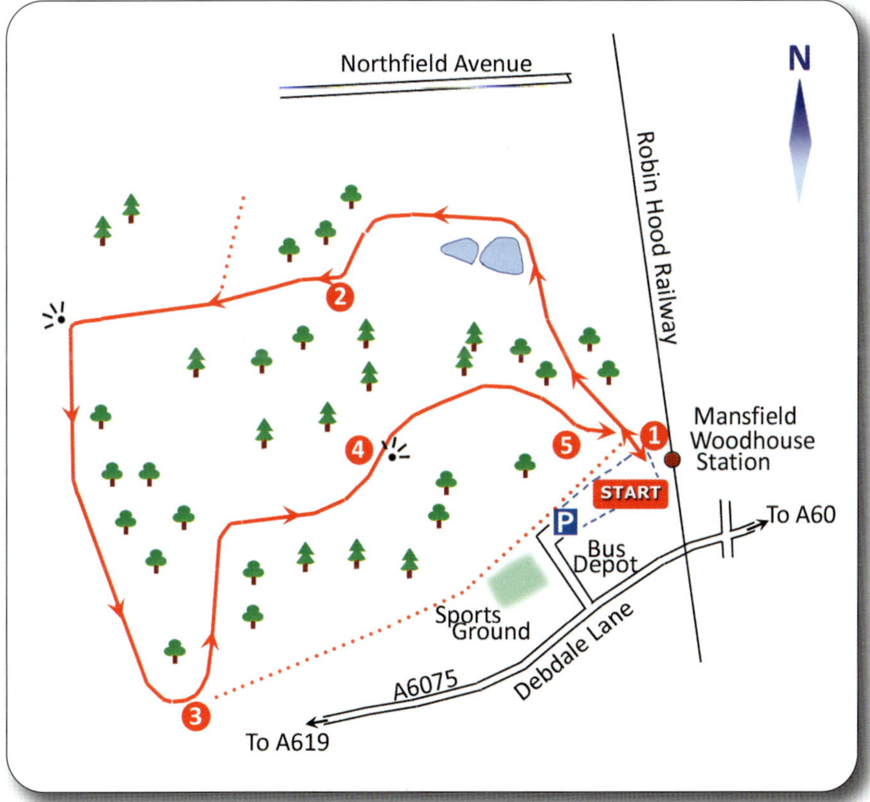

level, and follow the path round a large pond. Continue along this path which eventually comes to a T-junction.

2 At the T-junction turn right and keep on this wide path following the track round the old spoil heaps, passing a large viewpoint wall on the right. The path bends to the left and continues down a long straight to reach a left-hand bend.

3 Directly after the bend, turn left and climb a steep grassy path. At the top turn right onto a wide path. Take the next path on the left which soon reaches a junction just before the second viewpoint wall.

4 Take the right-hand path which bends to the right and eventually reaches another path coming from the right.

5 At the junction turn left down a steep grassy path to reach the noticeboards. Take the steps back to the car park.

Heading off from Mansfield Woodhouse.

Ollerton Pit Wood

The path near the lake.

This is a hidden gem of a dog walk close to a sprawling colliery village. Most local people think of Ollerton as being split into 'new' and 'old'. The old Ollerton was originally known as Alreton, or Allerton, meaning 'farm among the alders' and is situated at a very busy crossroads on the old York to London road. Its location led, in medieval times, to the village becoming a meeting place for officials, and later the two coaching inns, the White Hart and the Hop Pole were established. For many years the main occupation of Ollerton was hop growing and there were hop fields all along the River Maun from as early as 1691. A weekly hop market was held in the village.

'New' Ollerton grew up around the colliery which opened in 1923. Few people realise that behind the village is a quiet nature walk round the former spoil heaps of Ollerton Colliery which closed in 1994. The site was landscaped between 1995 and 1997 and is now managed by Nottinghamshire County

Council and the Forestry Commission. It has become a wonderful natural paradise for birds, butterflies and invertebrates.

When the mine closed it was replaced with the Sherwood Energy Village. The E-centre building which manages the site was opened in 2006 and was built with a high standard of sustainability. The building has a ground-source heat pump, under-floor heating, a natural ventilation system and solar panels on a green roof. The village has won many awards and is visible from the top of the walk.

Terrain

Well-maintained stony tracks. There is a small fenced-off lake. On the north side there is a wet area with muddy ditches at the side of the path. There is one short but steep ascent and one long gradual descent.

Where to park

Free parking at the Ollerton Pit Wood car park (GR: SK 668674). **OS map:** Explorer 270 Sherwood Forest.

How to get there

From the A614 Nottingham to Ollerton road, take the A616 at Ollerton roundabout signed for Newark. After leaving Ollerton the road goes over a disused railway. Take the next left turn signed for Boughton (just before entering Wellow). Go under two railway bridges and the entrance to the car park is on the right.

Nearest refreshments

Drive back to the Ollerton roundabout where there is a selection of 'fast food' outlets, including a good fish and chip café with outside tables, or on the A616 Sheffield road you will find **Green Hut Café** which is open daily (except Wednesdays) from 7 am to 2 pm. Postcode NG22 9DR.

Dog factors

Distance: 3 miles
Road walking: None
Livestock: None, but there are fenced off areas where heritage sheep graze.
Stiles: None
Nearest vets: Portland House Veterinary Group, Ollerton. ☎ 01623 860138.

The Walk

1 Walk to the south end of the car park and follow the path round to the large noticeboards. Turn right towards the railway embankment. The path bends to the left with the railway embankment on your right. Pass the small lake on your left, the path now bends to the left, round the lake to reach a T-junction.

2 Turn right taking the wide path which eventually bends to the left downhill with embankments on either side of the path. Please be aware that there are muddy ditches along the side of the path.

3 At the end of the straight before the green barrier turn left up a steep hill.

There is a seat halfway up the hill with excellent views northwards. Look for the steam from Cottam Power Station on the River Trent.

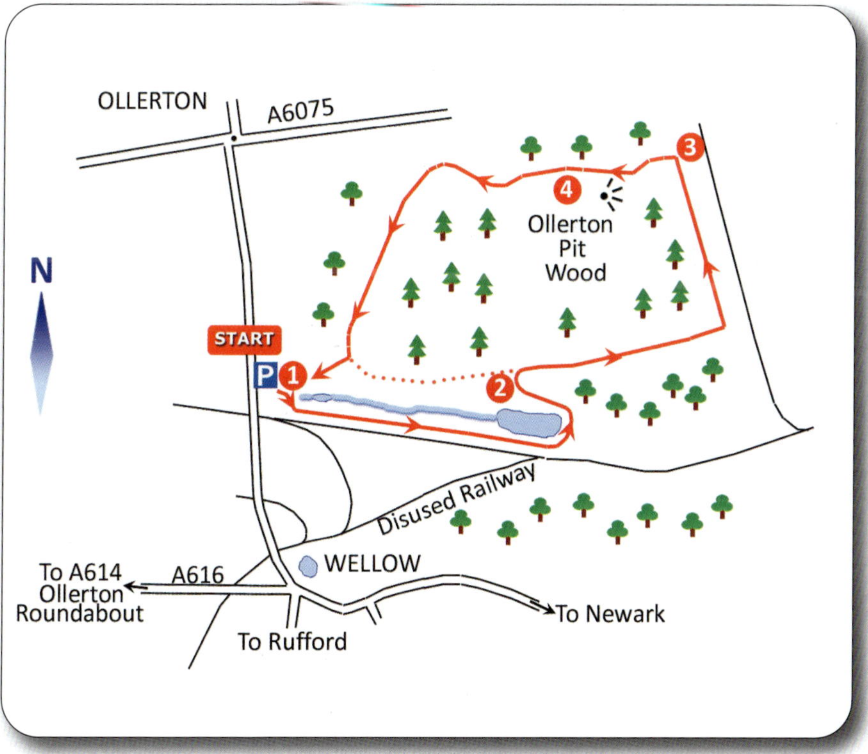

4 Continue past the viewpoint on the left and the beacon on the right which was used in the millennium celebrations. The path goes downhill to a large rock. Keep straight on back to the large display boards and continue to the car park.

Taking a rest at the Colliery Stone.

9

Vicar Water

Looking down on Vicar Pond.

A **panoramic walk with exceptional views** and a treat for nature lovers. On a warm spring day you are rewarded with the song of the skylark or the sight of the common blue butterfly searching for a mate amongst the bird's-foot trefoil. Later in the year there are lapwings, bee orchids and common lizards to be seen. The route then follows a disused railway line with broad-bodied chasers and damselflies sunning themselves on the gorse. Watch out for purple hairstreak butterflies with their silver undersides darting about in the tops of the oaks in late July, or latticed heath moths enjoying the purple heather on the embankment.

This is a really good walk for energetic dogs who love exploring, and you can exercise your ball-throwing ability. Although not a long walk, there is so much to see it can easily occupy a morning or afternoon.

Dog factors

Distance: 3 miles
Road walking: None
Livestock: None on the walk, but there are heritage sheep in fenced-off fields next to the walk.
Stiles: One. There is a hole in the fence for dogs to pass through next to the stile, if you prefer there is an alternative route back to the car park as this is close to the end of the walk and also avoids one of the steep ascents. There are two large gates which are easy to open.
Nearest vets: McPherson Veterinary Clinic, Rainworth. ☎ 01623 798050.

Terrain

Mostly along well-maintained stony tracks. There are two short but steep ascents to the top of the old spoil heaps. The disused railway track has been recently resurfaced and is used by fast moving cyclists.

Where to park

Vicar Water Country Park car park (there is a small voluntary donation parking charge). (GR: SK 588627). **OS map:** Explorer 270 Sherwood Forest.

How to get there

From the A614 Nottingham to Doncaster road turn towards Edwinstowe on the B6034. At the traffic lights turn left onto the B6030. Follow the road through Kings Clipstone to Clipstone. Just before the parade of shops turn left signposted to Vicar Water Country Park. From the A60 Mansfield to Ravenshead road, take the B6030 through Forest Town to Clipstone. After the parade of shops turn right into the country park.

Nearest refreshments

The café at Vicar Water Country Park is run by **Rumbles**, an award-winning catering project designed to help adults with learning difficulties. Unfortunately, dogs are not allowed in the café, but there is pleasant seating outside in fine weather. They have a 'fish Friday' and Sunday carvery, although booking may be required. The café is open Tuesday to Sunday 10 am to 4 pm. Postcode NG21 9AA. ☎ 01623 424836. Alternatively, if you fancy a walk from Vicar Water to a pub for lunch, then follow Cycle Route 6 north-east from the park (1 ½ miles) where you will find the **Dog & Duck**. This is a dog-friendly pub serving anything from a sandwich to pub favourites.

Well-behaved dogs are allowed in the bar. The pub is open every day from 11.30 am onwards. Postcode NG21 9BT. ☎ 01623 822138.

The Walk

1 From the car park walk through the gap to **Vicar Water**, cross the bridge and turn left up the steep hill. At the top, turn left following the path gently upwards past a seat on the left until a gate is reached.

2 Go through the gate, carry straight on following the stony track which winds its way over the top of the old spoil heap and then downwards towards another gate. Go through the gate following the track downhill to a stile.

From the top, facing south, it is possible to see over the vast expanse of Sherwood Pines which is the largest woodland in the East Midlands. Mainly an activity wood there is an 8-mile off-road circular cycle/walking route for really active dogs and handlers. Turn round and look north over Clipstone, this whole area was a First World War training camp before the pit village was built. The camp housed 20 battalions of 1,000 men each and was closed in 1920. Beyond Clipstone look for a straight row of trees. This was the world-famous 'straight mile' where, after the camp closed, motorcycle speed trials were held. In 1924 the British road record was set at 111.1 mph in front of a crowd of over 12,000 people.

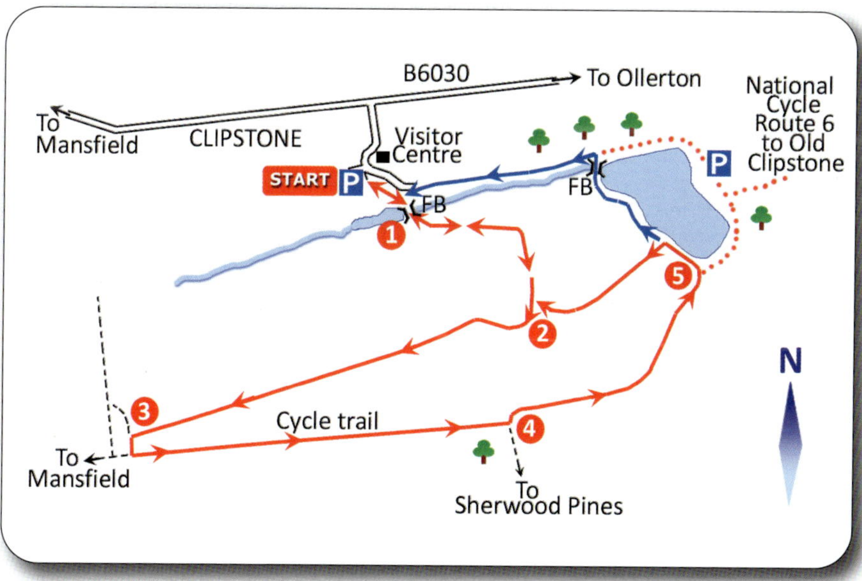

3 At the bottom of the hill turn left after the barrier and then immediately left again onto the newly resurfaced disused railway line. Follow this straight on for about a mile.

This is part of the Timberland Cycle Trail which runs from Mansfield to join up with the Sustrans Cycle Route 6 (York to Derby). The railway line ran from Crown Farm into the sidings at Clipstone Colliery which then continued north to the power stations on the River Trent. Please be aware there is a muddy ditch on the left where the water can turn green during hot weather.

4 After a gentle rise at the end of the railway line there is a green signpost marking the Route 6 Cycle Route. Turn left and follow the cycle route until it reaches **Vicar Pond**. Dogs should not be allowed in the water here as it is a fishing lake.

5 Keep to the left of **Vicar Pond**. Turn left over the stile taking the steep incline. *For an alternative route carry on round the pond until the tarmac road is reached, used by occasional cars. Turn left and follow the road back to the car park. Otherwise follow the track up the hill.*

There are views backwards towards what was the Clipstone Colliery yard. Look out for the golden hand glistening in the sun marking the cycle trail. At the top of the hill look for common purple orchids, and in late May you may see the dingy skipper, a rare butterfly in Nottinghamshire.

At the seat, turn right retracing your steps downhill to the car park.

Walking along the old railway line.

Stapleford Wood

Ready for the off!

This walk, on the border with Lincolnshire, is lovely all year round, but is best done in late spring when the banks of rhododendrons are in flower. Although these are now being actively cut back to allow the heather to regenerate, their large pink flowers are still a major attraction.

By the early 18th century, Stapleford Wood was owned by Lord Middleton, who also owned much of the surrounding land. In the 1920s the wood was bought by Trinity College, Cambridge, but it is now owned and managed by the Forestry Commission who purchased the land in 1945. It is an ancient woodland site which comprised mostly oak and birch. These were heavily worked at times, particularly with the demand from shipbuilding from the end of the 18th century and during the First World War, when much of the wood was felled. Although mature oaks are still present in significant numbers, especially on the woodland boundaries, much of the wood was replanted in the 1950s, predominantly with Scots and Corsican pine, together with a variety of other conifers.

A range of wildlife can be found along the forest rides, including speckled wood, brimstone and red admiral butterflies. In the trees can be seen grey squirrels, sparrow hawks, woodpeckers, gold crests and members of the tit family.

Terrain

Wide, level, woodland paths. The wood can be very wet and is sometimes prone to flooding.

Where to park

Free parking at the Stapleford Wood visitors car park (GR: SK 861566). **OS map:** Explorer 271 Newark-on-Trent.

How to get there

From Newark-on-Trent take the A17 signed to Sleaford. At the Coddington roundabout turn left onto Stapleford Lane signed for Stapleford. The car park is on the left, halfway through the wood.

Nearest refreshments

Drive back to the A17 and at the roundabout turn right and follow the road to the A46/A1 roundabout. On the right you will find the **Friendly Farmer Restaurant and Farm Shop**. Here dogs are very welcome at the covered outdoor tables. They open at 8 am for breakfast and continue with lunches using fresh produce, or on Sunday try the carvery. Afternoon teas include a lovely cake selection. The café is open until 5 pm all week. Postcode NG24 2NP. ☎ 01636 612461.

Dog factors

Distance: 4 miles
Road walking: There is about 300 yards on a farm road. One busy minor road is crossed twice. One quiet no through road is crossed.
Livestock: None
Stiles: None
Nearest vets: Minster Veterinary Centre, Newark.
☎ 01636 612906.

The Walk

1 From the car park walk into the wood away from the road to the right of the noticeboard until a wide track is reached. Turn left following the path for about 1 mile. The path eventually bends to the left before reaching a busy road.

2 Cross the road with care and continue along the wide path which bends round to the left. Follow the track for about 1 mile. On reaching a wooden barrier, cross the no through road with care. The path becomes narrower through the trees. Follow this path straight through another set of barriers and continue for

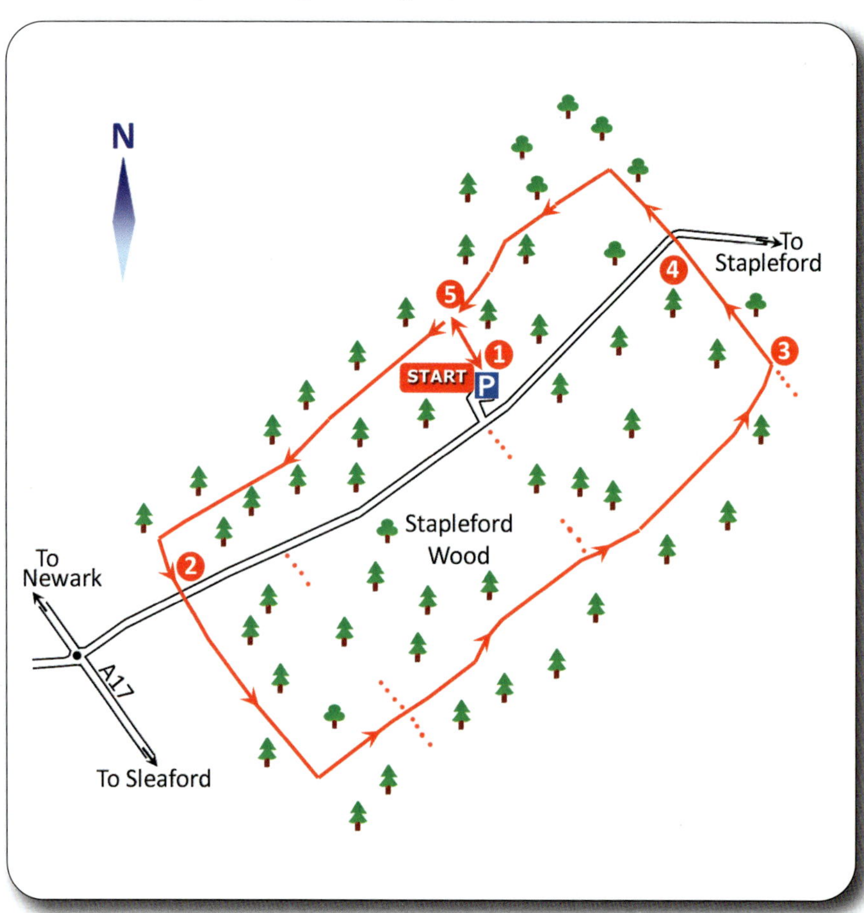

about ½ mile until you reach another wooden barrier with a tarmac road in front of you.

3 Turn left down the tarmac road to reach a busy minor road.

4 Go straight across the road past the houses towards a metal gate. Go through the narrow gap at the side of the gate. The path then bends to the left and crosses a small stream.

5 Halfway down the long straight, by a small white-topped post, turn left taking the path back to the car park.

Rhododendrons flowering at Stapleford.

Edingley &
the Southwell Trail

The view towards Edingley.

An easy short circular walk round quiet central Nottinghamshire. There is the bonus of an attractive pub halfway round the walk. From the car park it is possible to walk the whole seven miles of the Southwell Trail, a popular multi-use track, but our walk uses just one mile of it.

The Southwell Trail was once a busy branch line connecting Mansfield and Farnsfield to the Newark-on-Trent to Nottingham railway line. Completed in 1817, the single line was operated by the Midland Railway Company and transported people, coal and oil. The line was closed in 1965 and has now become a haven for wildlife. Birds, wild flowers, common lizards and butterflies are abundant in the hedgerows, cuttings and grassy embankments along the trail.

Terrain

Well-trodden grassy paths around Edingley which can be overgrown in summer. The Southwell Trail has a compacted earth track. This is also a popular cycle route. There are two small streams: the Edingley Beck and Cotton Mill Dyke.

Where to park

Free parking at the former Kirklington station (GR: SK 676566). **OS map:** Explorer 270 Sherwood Forest.

How to get there

From the A614 Nottingham to Ollerton road take the A617 signed for Newark-on-Trent. On entering Kirklington take the first right signed for Southwell. Just after leaving Kirklington take the first right, signed for Edingley. After 200 yards the road goes over a bridge, directly before this turn right and follow the narrow road into the car park.

Nearest refreshments

The **Old Reindeer** in Edingley is open from 12 noon until 11.30 pm, seven days a week. Dogs are welcome inside if the pub is not too busy, otherwise there are outside seating areas. The pub is well known for its fresh Whitby cod and haddock, but it also has an extensive snack menu. Postcode NG22 8BE. ☎ 01623 882253.

Dog factors

Distance: 2½ miles
Road walking: 300 yards, all on a pavement.
Livestock: The footpath passes down the side of one small field which sometimes has sheep grazing. The last time I walked through the field my dogs, on the lead, were within two yards of the sheep who completely ignored them.
Stiles: Three, all dog-friendly.
Nearest vets: Minster Veterinary Clinic, Southwell.
☎ 01636 812133.

The Walk

1 From the car park, walk right towards **Farnsfield** along the **Southwell Trail**. Before reaching the loading gauge turn left following the public footpath sign down several steps to a small meadow. **Edingley Beck** is on the left-hand side. Continue across three fields to reach an unmade road. Go straight across. Cross the next field to a stile. Cross the next field to another stile and then follow the path towards **Edingley**.

2 In the field just before the road keep to the left hand side to reach the bottom left hand corner where there is a gap in the hedge to reach the pavement.

On the trail,

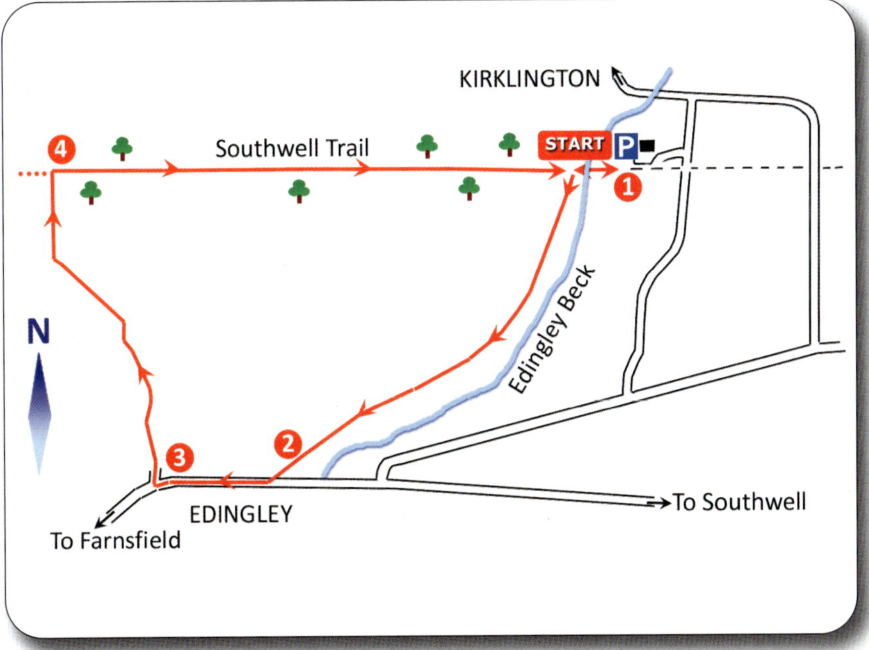

Turn right and walk down the pavement passing the **Old Reindeer** pub on the right.

3 At a footpath sign on the bend, turn right down an unmade track. At the end enter a field. Keep on the left-hand side of the field and then follow the footpath across the field to a gap in the hedge opposite. Pass through the gap and cross the next field following the footpath. Continue down the left-hand side of the field to reach the **Southwell Trail**.

4 Turn right and follow the trail for about 1 mile back to the car park.

Farndon Circular

Near Farndon Marina.

If you like boats, then this is the walk for you. Even dogs like a change from woodland and this route provides wide open vistas. The walk begins with the attractive Farndon Marina and the variety of craft moored there. Then we pass to a section of unspoilt river bank alive with butterflies, dragonflies and birds. Nature then gives way to industry again as the walk passes the new Staythorpe power station on the opposite side of the river. Then it's back to nature with the Averham weir.

You will need your binoculars to check out the water fowl and herons lined up along the weir edge like an army of soldiers guarding their stronghold. Eventually the path reaches meadows where wild flowers abound and dragonflies patrol. On a warm summer's day I enjoyed watching a banded demoiselle dragonfly here. After entering Farndon the walk passes over two village greens, one of which has a wonderful wild flower area.

Terrain

The walk is all on the level, with paths that are well trodden and wide. The river path can be subject to flooding.

Where to park

There is a free public car park next to the river in front of the Lock Keeper pub (GR: SK 768521). **OS map:** Explorer 271 Newark/Retford.

How to get there

From the A46 two miles south of Newark, turn into Main Street, Farndon, which then becomes Chapel Lane. Follow the road round a right-hand bend to the River Trent. The car park is on the left, next to the river.

Nearest refreshments

As you walk along the river, you pass through the car park of **Farndon Boathouse**. If you fancy a quality meal or just a coffee, then the Boathouse has several outdoor tables where dogs are welcome. Try the gourmet burgers with dripping chips. The restaurant is open from 12 noon to 2.30 pm and from 6 pm to 9.30 pm, seven days a week. Postcode NG24 3SX. ☎ 01636 676578.

The Walk

1 From the car park, walk towards the large chestnut tree and go through the **Farndon Boathouse** car park to reach the riverside path. Pass the **6th Newark Sea Scout Hut** and then continue over the **Farndon Marina Bridge** which was opened in 2002. Follow the riverside path for about 1½ miles with the **Trent** on your left. The path passes **Staythorpe power station** and **Averham weir**.

Dog factors

Distance: 3 miles
Road walking: A very short section in Farndon.
Livestock: None, although the riverside path goes through grass meadows. These have shown no signs of any livestock when I have walked through.
Stiles: None
Nearest vets: Minster Veterinary Centre, Newark.
☎ 01636 612906.

2 Eventually the path reaches a white gate. Pass through the gate to the next gate where there is a 'no fishing beyond this point' sign. Continue following the river towards an old windmill.

3 Go through the gate in the top left-hand corner of the field and directly turn right following a public footpath sign. Cross a driveway and continue until a road is reached. Follow the road to a mini roundabout. Turn right and follow an unmade road to reach a public footpath sign next to a dog-waste bin.

4 Turn left at the sign. On reaching the entrance to **Farndon Marina**, keep left going through a gate into a field. Walk through the field to reach another

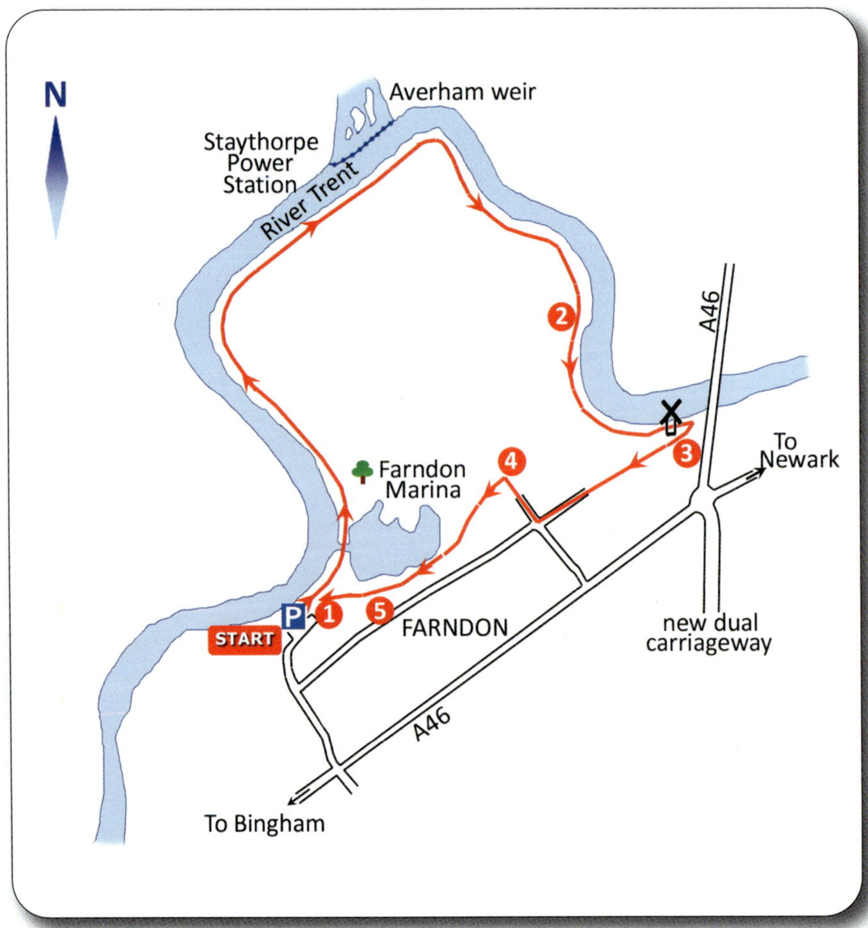

gate. There is a row of garages in front of you, pass these to reach a gap in the wall. Turn right and walk to a green footpath sign.

5 Turn left following a grassy path back to the riverside path. At the riverside turn left back to the car park.

The River Trent in early evening.

Blidworth Wood

Which way now?

If you have a friendly dog that loves to play with other dogs, or if you like to meet and greet other dog owners, then this is the walk for you. It is a really interesting, undulating, woodland walk and is very popular with walkers, cyclists and horse riders. The walk is all off-road and follows the marked Blue Trail round the mixed woodland.

Blidworth Wood was once known as Assarts Woods and was part of the ancient Royal Forest of Sherwood. The Forest Register of 1532 records that there were 128 red deer in Blidworth, fifteen of which were 'of antler'. Blidworth village was at that time fenced and gated against the deer. You may be lucky enough to catch sight of the deer. The wood is home to willow warblers and the elusive cuckoo in the spring, followed by spotted flycatchers in the summer. There are several pairs of tawny owls and numerous grey squirrels.

Terrain

Undulating woodland tracks following the Blue Trail markers. These can be a little indistinct at times.

Where to park

The walk starts from Longdale Lane car park (GR: SK 593525). **OS map:** Explorer 270 Sherwood Forest.

How to get there

From the A614 Nottingham to Ollerton road, turn left at the roundabout onto Londgale Lane, signposted to Ravenshead/Mansfield. The car park is halfway down a long straight on the right. From the A60 Nottingham to Mansfield road turn right onto Longdale Lane signposted for Lowdham. The car park is halfway down the long straight on the left.

Nearest refreshments

There is an excellent mobile catering unit in the car park which is open from 8 am, seven days a week, and does very good food, including beef burgers and ostrich burgers.

The Walk

1 From the car park walk northwards for about 30 yards passing under electricity cables and then turn right through a barrier, passing a blue post on the right. Continue uphill to reach a crossroads, go straight across. The path bends to the left and reaches another set of barriers. Go straight across, downhill.

Dog factors

Distance: 3 miles
Road walking: None
Livestock: The wood is used by horse riders.
Stiles: None
Nearest vets: McPherson Veterinary Clinic, Rainworth. ☎ 01623 798050.

Nottinghamshire – A Dog Walker's Guide

2 At the next barriers go straight on uphill. Near the top of the hill the path bends to the left. At the next junction turn right following the blue posts uphill. Near the top of the hill turn left at the barrier through the pine trees and continue to a T-junction. Turn right until a crossroads is reached.

3 Go straight across and down through the trees. Continue straight on at the next crossing onto a narrow track. After 20 yards take a left turn to reach the main driveway, turning right.

4 After 150 yards, turn left just after a blue post on the right. There is a mature conifer wood on the right and a younger plantation on your left. On reaching a crossroads turn left going slightly downhill. The path bends to the right and then to the left, with blue posts on the right. Follow this winding path through two wooden barriers to reach a wider path.

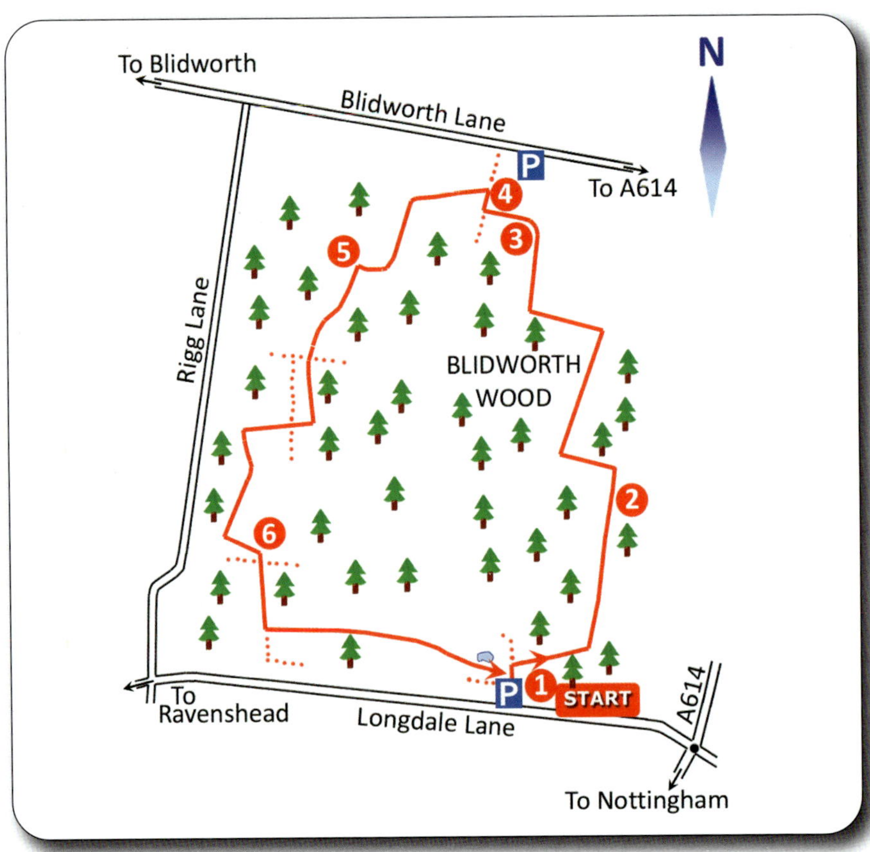

5 Go straight across onto a narrow uphill path round wood barriers. Just after the next barriers turn right at the T-junction and walk downhill to reach a main driveway. Go straight on and, after 200 yards, take a left-hand path round the barriers. The path climbs round another set of barriers.

6 At a small crossroads turn left to reach a junction of tracks. Take the broad path on the right downhill. At the bottom of the hill take the second woodland path on the left with a 'No horses' sign. Go round the barriers. At the junction of several paths, carry straight on round another set of barriers. Pass a small pond on the left keeping straight on here back to the car park.

Macey and Jake at point 4 of the walk.

Brierley Forest Country Park

Brierley Forest's dog-friendly visitor centre.

This interesting and lovely walk is well worth a visit just to see the glorious wild flower meadows. Brierley Country Park was created in 1992, mainly from the spoil heaps of Sutton Colliery between Huthwaite and Stanton Hill. Loving care and attention have allowed it to develop into a flourishing area for walking, with surprises round every corner. It became known as Brierley because many of the original miners came from Brierley Hill in the West Midlands.

There is a large pond known as Brierley Water, wetlands, old hedges and plenty of mixed woodland. As well as the wildlife interest, sculpture lovers are catered for with impressive designs along the walk based on the area's heritage, coal mining, railways and agriculture. The park is managed by Ashfield Council.

Terrain

Mostly well-maintained, compacted red ash or stony paths. As the walk circles the park there are no steep climbs. There is an unfenced golf course which runs next to the path on the last part of the walk.

Where to park

Free parking close to the visitor centre (GR: SK 472595). **OS map:** Explorer 269 Chesterfield/Alfreton.

How to get there

From Sutton-in-Ashfield town centre take the B6026 (Sutton Road) to Huthwaite. Follow the brown sign to the park down Skegby Road. The car park is at the bottom of the road on the right.

Nearest refreshments

The visitor centre has a café which is very dog-friendly. The sign on the door states 'Dogs on leads and muddy boots welcome'. Although there is not a vast array of choice, what is available is very reasonably priced. The café is open every day. Postcode NG21 2PL. ☎ 01623 550172.

The Walk

1 In the car park, face the visitor centre and turn right along a wide stony path, for about 100 yards. Pass the pit wheels from the former Sutton Colliery which closed in 1989. Please make sure your dog is on the lead at this point. Directly after passing the noticeboards turn right following the path with Brierley Water on your left.

Dog factors

Distance: 3 miles
Road walking: None
Livestock: None, but the success of ground-nesting birds in the park means that visitors are urged to keep their dogs on the lead near long grass during the nesting season (March to September). There may also be restrictions on where you can let your dog off-lead in the future. On no account should dogs be allowed in Brierley Water.
Stiles: None
Nearest vets: Thompsons Veterinary Surgery, Sutton-in-Ashfield.
☎ 01623 555460.

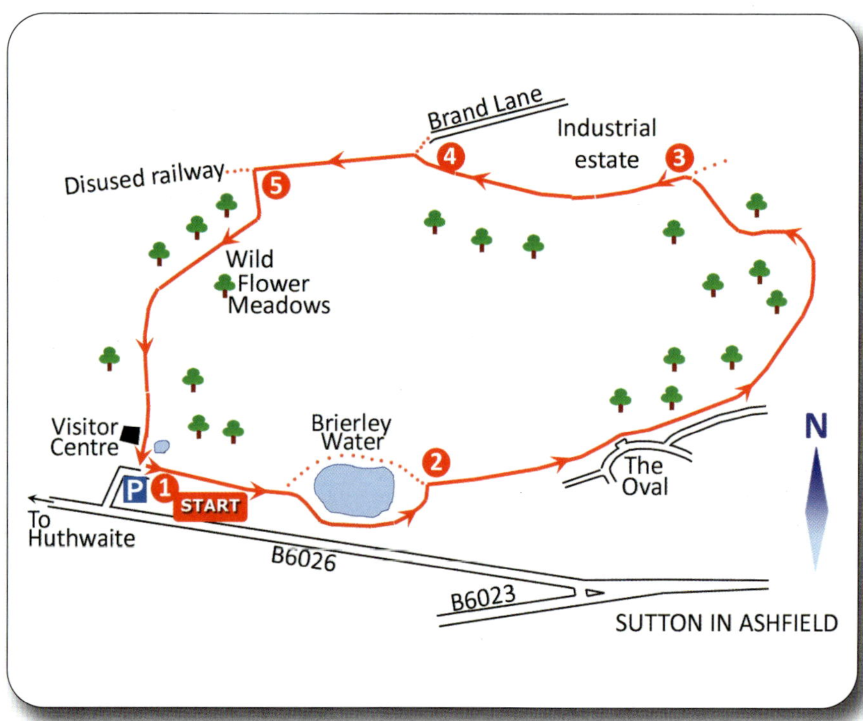

The Waters, which have been fenced off to protect birds were created by the damming of Rooley Brook. There is an impressive sculpture by Andrew McKeown at the end of the path on the left. Entitled 'Breaking the Mould' it depicts a giant seed that has emerged from a broken industrial mould, symbolising rebirth.

2 At the T-junction turn right and follow the path uphill to reach a crossroads. Go straight across following the signs for **Stoneyford Road**. Follow the winding path until a T-junction is reached.

3 Turn left following the signs for **Stanton Hill** and the visitor centre. Notice the wild flower bank on the left which is alive with butterflies and bees in late spring and summer. Look out for small orange skippers, common blues and chocolate ringlet butterflies. Continue until a crossroads is reached.

4 At the crossroads keep right and then turn left onto a wider track. This was the railway line for the colliery. There is a Nottinghamshire County Council sign for the Brierley Branch on your right and a sign reading 'Silverhill Trail 1 mile'.

5 Turn left at the sign which reads 'Brierley Forest Park ¾ mile'. Take the second path on the right signed to the Visitor Centre. There are several paths on the right to the Hardwick Viewpoint which is a very short detour if you have time. Follow this past more wild flower meadows created in 1995–6. Look out for yellow rattle, wild carrot and lesser trefoil, in season. Pass a stone seat on the right, with poetry by Benjamin Zephaniah. Carry straight on to the next junction then bend slightly to the left to the visitor centre. The car park is in front of you.

Well, I'm going this way!

Moorgreen

The timeless landscape at Moorgreen.

This is a walk I have enjoyed for several years. Not only is it a lovely walk but you can imagine that the landscape has not changed much since D.H. Lawrence trod the same paths. There is one very modern exception, of course, the M1, which the route crosses twice: once via a bridge, where I find it quite pleasing to see the vehicles speeding past while I am enjoying a countryside walk in the fresh open air. The second crossing is through an underpass which has recently been extended to accommodate the widening of the road.

Because of the limited parking close to Moorgreen Reservoir, the walk begins from the car park at Colliers Wood. This wood was created around the old spoil heaps of Moorgreen Colliery and there is a pleasant walk of about a mile round the wood from the car park if you are feeling less energetic.

The history of Moorgreen Colliery can be traced back to 1680. It was owned by Barber, Walker & Co. who, by the 20th century, had a virtual monopoly on the pits in the Eastwood area. They had an extensive private railway system which connected various collieries. The spoil from Moorgreen Colliery would be taken every day to Watnall Brickworks on the other side of the M1 for use in the production of 'common' bricks. These bricks were not made of clay but of crushed spoil from the colliery. They were similar to the breeze blocks we use today. The railway ran from the other side of the B600, opposite the entrance to the colliery at the bottom of Engine Lane.

Terrain

The stream at the far end of the reservoir can be muddy. There is a long, fairly steep ascent, although there are plenty of seats along the walk. All the paths are wide and well used.

Where to park

Although there is a small lay-by on the B600 near Moorgreen Reservoir, there is ample free parking at Colliers Wood (GR: SK 481481). **OS maps:** Explorer 260 Nottingham and Explorer 269 Chesterfield. The walk begins on map 260.

How to get there

From junction 27 of the M1, take the A608 signed to Heanor. Keep left following the B600 to Nottingham. After passing the head of Moorgreen Reservoir, take the next right, signed to Moorgreen Industrial Park and Colliers Wood (Engine Lane). The car park is on the left.

Nearest refreshments

There is a picnic area at **Colliers Wood**, close to the car park.

Dog factors

Distance: 5 miles
Road walking: There is about ¼ mile from the car park to the start of the walk along a busy roadside pavement and back. There is also a small section of track which is used by occasional traffic.
Livestock: None
Stiles: None
Nearest vets: Lawrence Veterinary Centre Ltd., Eastwood. ☎ 01773 769298.

Nottinghamshire – A Dog Walker's Guide

The Walk

1 Walk out of the car park and turn right, back to the B600. Turn left and cross the road onto the pavement. Walk along the pavement for about ¼ mile. At the information boards, facing away from the main road, take the road on the left signed 'Beauvale House'. There is also a public bridleway sign for Felley Mill.

Beauvale House is a Grade II listed building set back in High Park Wood with an impressive 90-ft tower. In D.H. Lawrence's time it was owned by Lord and Lady Cowper and he would visit the housekeeper, the aunt of a school friend, during times when their lordships were away. The fictional family home in The White Peacock *is said to be based on Beauvale House. It is also thought that the gamekeeper's hut near the house was used in* Lady Chatterley's Lover. *The house and grounds are now private.*

2 Walk up the drive, with a wooden fence on either side and the reservoir visible through the trees on the left. When the road forks, go left onto a track with a wooden fence on the left and a wire fence on the right.

Moorgreen Reservoir was constructed around 1796 to supply water to the Erewash, Nottingham and Cromford canals. It is believed that D.H. Lawrence used its setting

Macey enjoying a cooling dip.

in two books, as Nethermere in The White Peacock *and Willey Water in* Women in Love. *In fact, the drowning in Women in Love was based on an actual incident at the reservoir in 1892. When full, the reservoir is a mile in length.*

3 Just before a small stone bridge, turn right to reach a three-way junction. There is a large pile of rubble on the right. Take the middle path which climbs steadily upwards for about ½ mile with open fields on either side. As the path becomes steeper there is a welcome bench where it is possible to rest and admire the view down the valley. Note the message on the bench! Continue along the track past **America Farm** and over the bridge above the M1.

4 At the next junction turn right. After passing several houses, continue to a metal gate with an opening on the right. Follow the wide track (**Kennel Lane**) with a wood on the right and fields on the left for about ½ mile.

5 The path slopes downwards to reach a junction. Turn right and follow the path under the M1. Just after the underpass, keep straight on when the main track bends to the left. Emerge from the woodland to a wonderful view across the valley. Underwood church is visible on the horizon. Follow this path downhill for about ½ mile until a signpost is reached.

6 At the signpost keep left, following the public footpath sign round the edge of the field. Turn right at the next signpost, following the path through a gap in the hedge back onto the reservoir path. Turn left following the path back to the B600. At the main road turn left and walk down the pavement, crossing the road to take the first road on the right back to the car park.

16

Gunthorpe & the River Trent

The riverside path.

This walk from a very popular location is suitable for dogs who enjoy being on the lead. The scenery goes from arable fields to a wide riverside walkway. The River Trent is a busy waterway and there are usually canal boats and pleasure boats to be seen.

The Trent was an important route for the Romans, who called it Tristantona. In the 8th century the river was known as Treonte. The Danes later sailed up the Trent and settled at Gunthorpe. The Old Gunthorpe Bridge Company built a large iron toll bridge over the river in 1875 at a ford where a ferry had operated since Roman times. The 1925 Gunthorpe Bridge Act allowed the Council to buy the owners out, demolish the bridge and replace it with the present one. This was reputed to be the first toll bridge in the country to later become free to cross.

The Trent is now one of Britain's longest navigable rivers. The Trent Ketch, which was built solely for use on the Newark Navigation, has now been replaced by modern craft.

Terrain

The whole of the route is well-used, with wide grassy verges and well-defined footpaths. During prolonged periods of rain the Trent is liable to flooding which may make the route impassable.

Where to park

There is a free public car park opposite the Unicorn Hotel on the riverside close to the bridge (GR: SK 683437). **OS map:** Explorer 260 Nottingham.

How to get there

Gunthorpe is on the A6097 which can be reached from the A612 Nottingham to Southwell road, or from the A46 Leicester to Newark road.

Nearest refreshments

There are several restaurants, cafés and bistros in Gunthorpe. **The Unicorn Hotel** ☎ 0115 966 3612 has a sign which says 'We love Dogs'. There is a seating area round the back for well behaved dogs on leads.

Dog factors

Distance: 3½ miles
Road walking: About ¼ mile on pavements in Gunthorpe village and a short section in Caythorpe, including about 100 yards on a roadside grass verge.
Livestock: The grass meadows at the side of the Trent usually have cows grazing. They are so used to people and dogs that they rarely show any interest in them.
Stiles: None
Nearest vets: Buttercross Vet Centre, Bingham. ☎ 01949 837571.

Gunthorpe Lock on the River Trent.

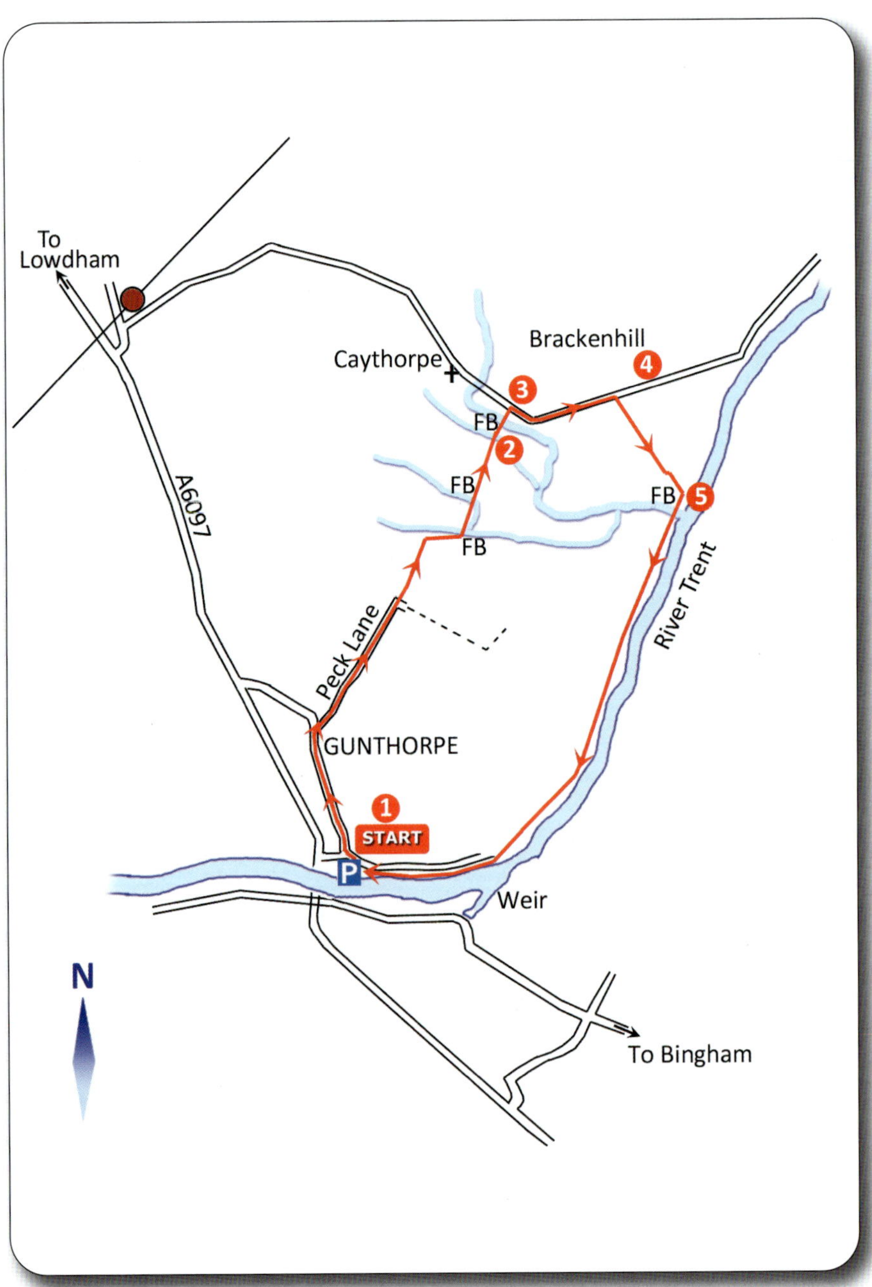

To
Lowdham
Caythorpe
Brackenhill
3
4
FB
2
FB
FB
5
FB
A6097
River Trent
Peck Lane
GUNTHORPE
1
START
P
Weir
N
To Bingham

The Walk

1 From the car park take **Main Street** to the left of the **Unicorn Hotel**. Continue up this road for about ¼ mile. Turn right down **Peck Lane** by the Public Footpath sign passing the houses and continuing down a tarmac road.

2 When the road goes right, continue straight ahead onto a grassy field verge following a footpath sign. On reaching a yellow-topped post at the field edge, turn right and continue halfway down the field. Turn left to cross a plank bridge. Go straight across two further bridges to reach a metal gate. Please ensure that dogs are on leads at this point. Cross the meadow to reach a further metal gate. Pass through this into a garden, following the Public Footpath signs. Keep to the left of the outbuildings and follow the path to the road. The house on the left is the **Old Water Mill** which was built in 1749.

3 On reaching the road, turn right, crossing with care onto the pavement. Follow the road out of **Caythorpe** towards **Hoveringham**. After the pavement ends, cross over to the wider grass verge.

4 On reaching a bridleway sign, turn right and follow the path down the field side to reach a metal gate. Go through the gate (beware, the fast flowing River Trent is in front of you) and continue over the meadow towards the river path.

5 Turn right following the path for about 1 mile until **Gunthorpe Lock** is reached.

Gunthorpe Lock, which is lock No. 7 on the Trent, was constructed to hold four Trent ketches and was originally operated manually. It was mechanised in 1959. The Bottom Lock gate weighs 14,600 kg – equivalent to five adult female elephants. It would take about 14 hours for a ketch to reach Hull from Gunthorpe.

Go through the gate past the lock and walk along the riverside path to the car park.

Bestwood Country Park

A crisp winter morning at Bestwood.

This almost completely off-road circular walk around the hilly woods of Bestwood Country Park is very popular with the dog walkers of Nottingham as it is a green haven amongst the urban sprawl of the city. The walk starts at the car park in Bestwood Village which is where the old colliery workings were situated. In 1872, the 10th Duke of St Albans leased some land to John Lancaster who sank a mine shaft here. As the mine expanded, the village also grew to accommodate the workers and their families, with the first colliery houses being built in 1876. Soon the Bestwood Coal and Iron Village was established. The colliery closed in 1967, although the winding house can still be seen. This listed building, along with the headstocks, is unique in that it has a steam-driven vertical winding engine.

Steeped in history, the country park encloses the woods which formed part of the southern end of Sherwood Forest. It was a royal hunting ground and is mentioned in the Domesday Book. Bestwood was also a favourite haunt of Charles II and he enjoyed staying here with his mistress, Nell Gwynne. She acquired the estate in 1687 and her son, by the king, became the 1st Duke of St Albans. The Bestwood Lodge Hotel was built in 1864 on the site of the original medieval hunting lodge.

The 650-acre country park offers many diverse landscapes, including heathland, water meadows, woodland, grassland and formal gardens, which produce a haven for wildlife. There is also a small children's play area and an education centre.

Terrain

The first half of the walk is very hilly, with some short steep ascents and descents. The walk is then mostly level. The paths are generally very good and well-defined.

Where to park

There is a car park with a height restriction barrier (2 m) on Park Road in Bestwood Village (GR: SK 556475). **OS map:** Explorer 260 Nottingham.

How to get there

From Nottingham, take the A611 towards Hucknall. Turn right onto the B683, signed to Bestwood Village. Take a right turn into Park Road following the brown signs for Bestwood Country Park. The car park is just round the left-hand bend on the right.

Nearest refreshments

Return to the B683 and turn right. Continue straight along this road into Papplewick (about 2 miles). Just before the crossroads on the right you will find the car park for the **Griffins Head**. Here dogs are welcome either indoors or outdoors. The pub is open from 12 noon and serves a variety of hot and cold food until 8 pm. Postcode NG15 8EN. ☎ 0115 9633 672.

Dog factors

Distance: 4 miles
Road walking: The walk crosses the quiet main country park road twice.
Livestock: None, but some of the paths are used by horse riders.
Stiles: None
Nearest vets: Buckley House Vets, Hucknall. ☎ 0115 9527 271.

Nottinghamshire – A Dog Walker's Guide

The Walk

1 From the car park, go through the barrier towards the winding wheel. Keep to the left, with a large display board on your right. At the triangular junction, keep left following the wide path. Just before you reach a board which says 'Bigwood 20 mins', turn left on a narrow uphill path, with a 'horse trail' sign. Continue up the hill, keeping to the left halfway up, taking some wooden steps. Eventually fields can be seen on the left. Carry straight on downhill passing a small children's play area on the right. The path becomes tarmac with the Field Study Centre on the right. Please be aware that the main park road is ahead.

2 Turn right at the main drive towards **Alexandra Lodges**. Just before the Lodges keep left, going uphill. Go round a wooden barrier and pass a sign saying 'No horses on trail'. There is also a sign for Colliers Path. Continue up the hill until a field is visible on the left-hand side.

3 Take the second path on the right opposite a large 'horse trail' sign and just after a small post with the number 16 carved in the top. The path goes steeply down and up until the main park road is reached.

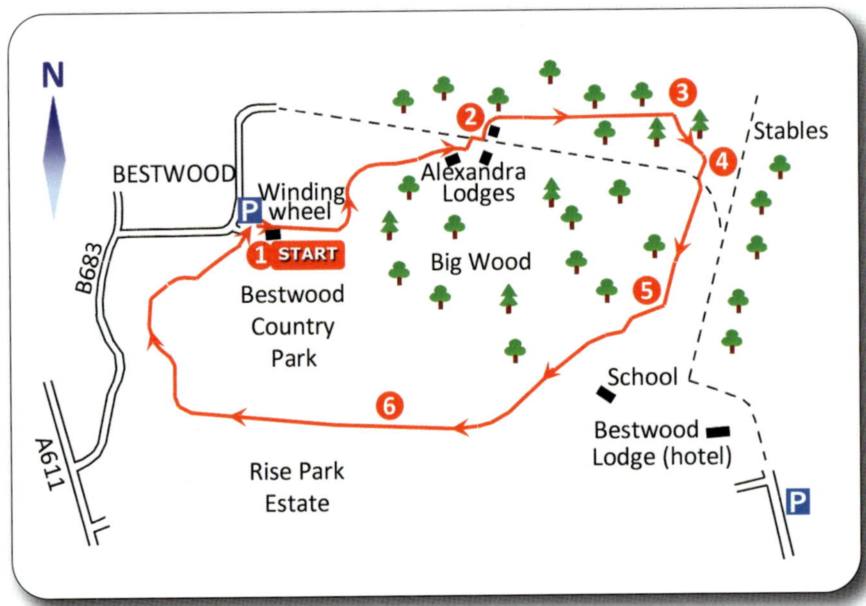

4 At the main park road, turn left and take the second path on the right just before the barrier. This has a 'No horses' sign. Follow this path until a T-junction at the park edge is reached. Turn right and continue along this path to a crossroads, there is a sign on the left reading 'Woodman's Path'.

5 At the crossroads, turn left and then keep left again at the next junction of paths. There are high black railings on the left of the track. The track passes a school playing field and continues with houses on the left and a steep drop on the right. Follow this wide path for about ½ mile to a crossroads just after an information board.

6 At the crossroads go straight over down a path, with a wide grass verge on the left and houses beyond the verge. There is a hedge on the right. Stay on this path for a further mile as it twists through a series of small bends. Eventually, just before the Engine House, there is a left hand path which reaches an open green space and sports area. The path bends to the right over the green to the winding house, turn left here back to the car park.

Springtime in the country park.

Cotgrave Forest

The crossroads in the forest.

This is truly a walk for those who don't mind getting their boots and dogs muddy. Wellingtons are the most appropriate form of footwear especially during wet weather and even in high summer some of the paths can be extremely muddy, particularly around the streams. 'Why do the walk?' – you may well ask. Well, there are the far reaching views of Nottingham and the Trent valley, the joy of walking through ancient woodland, and it's fun!

Cotgrave Forest is now in private hands and there are signs at the side of the bridleways indicating that 'shooting' is taking place. It is therefore advisable to place dogs on leads through the woodland if they have a tendency to run off. All that my dogs are interested in is paddling in the

Dog factors

Distance: 4½ miles
Road walking: ¼ mile in Clipston village
Livestock: None, although some of the bridleways are used by horse riders.
Stiles: None
Nearest Vets: Buttercross Veterinary Centre, Cotgrave. ☎ 01159 893711.

streams, they wouldn't know what a pheasant was if they saw one sitting at the side of the path.

Terrain

Undulating throughout. The paths in the forest section are generally good with some muddy places around the streams. Wolds Lane and Mill Lane, which are public bridleways, can be rutted and extremely muddy.

Where to park

The best parking is on Laming Gap Lane where there is plenty of space on the verge. Please make sure that your car is securely locked (GR: SK 646322).
OS map: Explorer 260 Nottingham.

How to get there

From Nottingham, take the A606, Melton Mowbray road, towards the A46 (the Fosse Way). About ¼ mile after the last turning for Normanton-on-the-Wolds, turn left into Laming Gap Lane. (This is now signed as a no through road due to the new A46). Follow the road past farm buildings and park around a sharp right-hand bend.

Nearest refreshments

Unfortunately there are none suitable nearby so why not bring a picnic.

The Walk

1 Follow the bridleway sign uphill towards **Cotgrave Forest** keeping straight on at the green metal barrier with the main forest on your right. Walk downhill until the path bends to the right to reach a junction. Turn left, still downhill, and cross a stream. At the next junction continue straight on, following a public

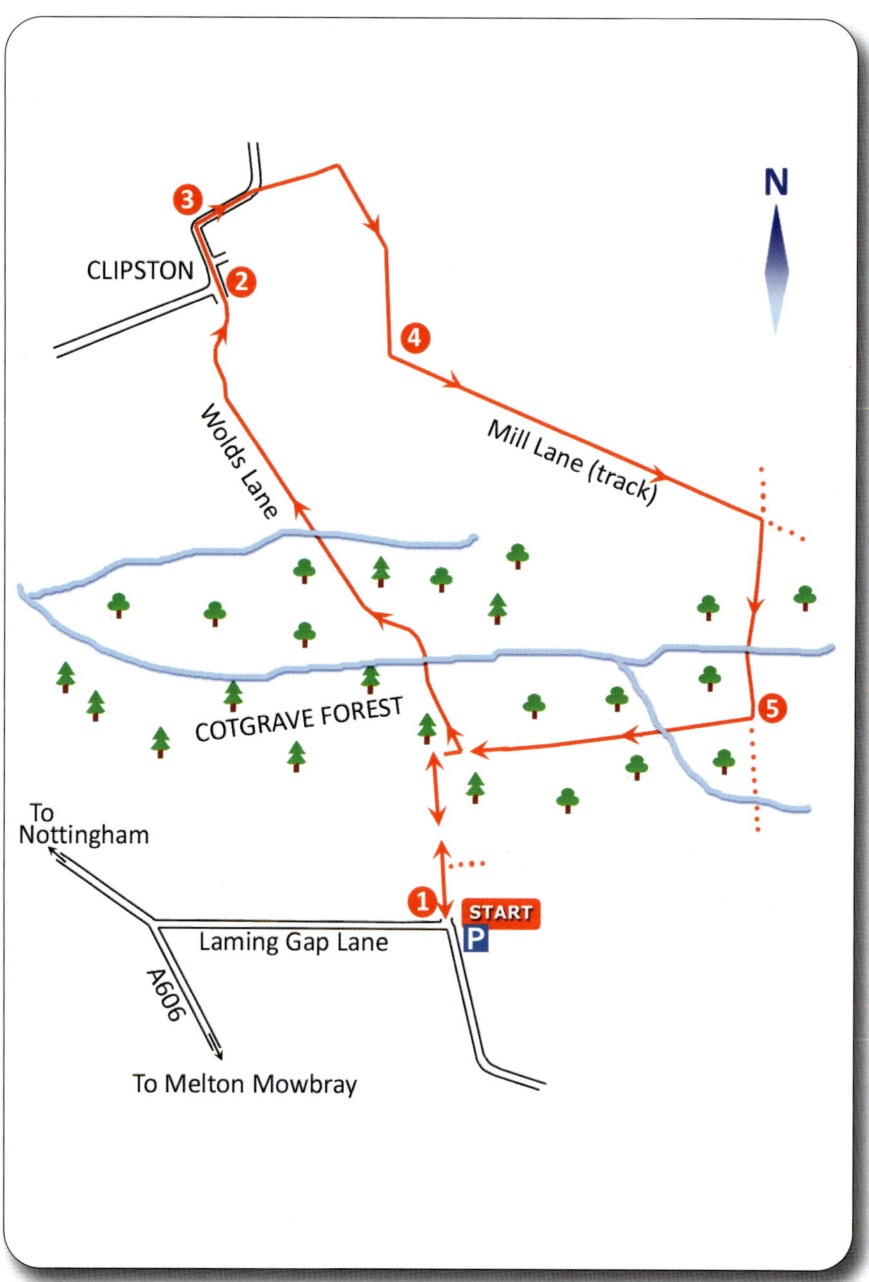
N
3
CLIPSTON
2
4
Wolds Lane
Mill Lane (track)
COTGRAVE FOREST
5
To
Nottingham
1
START
P
Laming Gap Lane
A606
To Melton Mowbray

footpath sign. After crossing another stream the track leaves the forest (**Wolds Lane**) and continues to the village of **Clipston**.

Harkers Farm Shop is on the right as you enter the village. It was established in 1954 and sells quality products including 35 different varieties of sausage. The shop is open Tuesday to Saturday.

2 Continue straight on up **Gilliver Lane**, ignoring **Church Gate** on the left and the road to **Manor Farm** on the right.

Church Gate is recorded in documents as being in the possession of Earl Manvers of Thoresby Hall, Nottinghamshire, in 1585.

In the forest.

3 The road bends to the right and goes slightly downhill to reach a sharp left-hand bend. Carry straight on here through a gate following a restricted byway sign. The path soon reaches an open field. Keep straight down the side of the field turning right, following the field verge uphill with the open field on your left.

4 At the top of the hill carry straight on down a rutted farm track (**Mill Lane**) with a hedge on your right. Keep on this path for about ¾ mile to a crossroads. Turn right, slightly downhill. Cross a stream and then climb again to reach a bridleway sign.

5 At the sign turn right, back into **Cotgrave Forest**, going round a green barrier. Follow this track for about ½ mile through the woodland, at the junction of tracks keep straight on, the path goes round the left-hand bend, continue uphill and back to your car.

Attenborough Wetlands

The attractive visitor centre at Attenborough.

Although this is a walk where it is advisable for dogs to be on the lead due to the large number of ground-nesting birds and waterfowl, it is such an interesting walk for dogs and their families that Attenborough Nature Reserve had to be included. One of the most important nature conservation sites in the East Midlands, the walk can easily be shortened or indeed lengthened to include Beeston Marina.

The area was once an expanse of wet grassland alongside the River Trent. In 1929, sand and gravel extraction began in order to provide materials for building and infrastructure in the Nottingham area. This ceased in 1967. After a period of restoration, most of the soil has been returned to the water-filled pits, creating a patchwork of lakes and islands. The area was designated a Site of Special Scientific Interest (SSSI) in 1982. The 365 acres provide an extensive variety of habitats for waterfowl and other important wildlife species. You can expect to see wild flower grasslands and scrub, reed beds, marshland, ponds and ancient willow/alder areas.

The site is now run by Nottinghamshire Wildlife Trust in partnership with Broxtowe Borough Council and the site owners, Cemex. The funding was eventually secured for an eco-friendly building on the site, which is now the visitor centre and café. The building is on the flood plain of the River Trent and was constructed to be durable, super-insulated and use renewable energy.

Terrain

The paths are compacted and wide but can be muddy and flooded during periods of extensive rain.

Where to park

There is a large car park close to the visitor centre (GR: SK 515339). The parking fee (£2.00 donation at the time of writing) is used to help maintain the reserve. **OS map:** Explorer 260 Nottingham.

How to get there

From junction 25 of the M1 take the A52 towards Nottingham. At the first junction turn right onto the B6003 signed for Toton. At the first traffic lights turn left. After passing Chetwynd Barracks turn right at the roundabout. Go straight across at the traffic lights and then straight across at the next roundabout signed for the Attenborough Nature Reserve. From Nottingham take the A52 out of Nottingham. After passing through Beeston turn left signed for Chilwell Retail Park and Attenborough Nature Reserve. Go straight across the roundabout towards the reserve.

Nearest refreshments

Although not accessible for dogs, the **visitor centre café** provides light meals and warm drinks. It is open Monday to Friday 10 am to 5 pm and weekends and bank holidays 9 am to 6 pm. There are plenty of places to have picnics around the reserve. Postcode NG9 6DY. ☎ 0115 972 1777.

Dog factors

Distance: 2 miles
Road walking: A short section in Attenborough village.
Livestock: None
Stiles: None
Nearest vets: Vets4Pets, Nottingham. ☎ 0115 9225 357.

The Walk

① From the car park rooundabout, face the **River Trent** with the Visitor Centre on your right, and walk straight ahead over the bridge following the path. Go round a barrier, pass a bird hide on your left and continue to reach a signpost. Keep left following the sign for 'Riverside Path to Beeston Marina & Nottingham'. Follow the path at the side of the River Trent until a path on the left is reached. There is an information board with 'Bird Migration' on the right and a green seat on the left.

The reed beds and scrub here are home to a variety of birds, including sedge warbler, garden warbler, meadow pipit and common whitethroat.

② Turn left, go round the green barrier and continue straight on following the path with lakes on either side. The path crosses over a bridge to reach a green open space.

3 Go straight on at the signpost towards **Attenborough Village**. There is a brick wall on the right and green railings on the left. On reaching the road keep left following the pavement. Take the first road on the left, **Church Lane** and pass St Mary the Virgin Church.

4 Take the next left path signed 'Public Bridleway, Attenborough Nature Reserve'. Please note the plaque on the wall dedicated to General Henry Ireton, son-in-law of Oliver Cromwell. At the next signpost keep right and follow the path back to the car park.

Is it left or right?!

Ruddington & the Great Central Railway

The wonderful countryside at Ruddington.

Here is a great family walk which, of course, also includes the four-legged member, as there is something for everyone. There's an extensive play area for the children, industrial heritage for transport enthusiasts, outstanding views and a lovely nature reserve. What about the most important member of the family? Although some areas of the nature reserve are out of bounds or 'on-lead' only, there are plenty of places for a good run and lots of chances to meet other doggy friends.

Rushcliffe Country Park was created around the site of a decommissioned Second World War munitions factory. The factory was built in 1940 and comprised over 200 buildings. After 1945 when the site was no longer required, it was used for auctioning redundant ex-military vehicles and equipment. It finally closed in 1983. In 1989 work began by Nottinghamshire County Council to clear the rubble which was then used to landscape the park.

Part of the park became the Nottingham Transport Heritage Centre which has an impressive collection of classic buses and steam trains in various gauges.

The country park has over five miles of pathways, wild flower meadows and over 400 species of trees.

Terrain

Well-maintained paths in the park. The field verge and path at the side of the railway can be overgrown and wet in prolonged periods of heavy rain.

Where to park

There is a large car park at Rushcliffe Country Park, with a machine for suggested donations of £1 to help with the upkeep of the park. The gates are open from 8 am, with a closing time displayed on the entrance gate (GR: SK 575322). **OS map:** Explorer 260 Nottingham.

How to get there

Take the A60 south from Nottingham, signed for Ruddington and Loughborough. On leaving Ruddington turn right at the last roundabout which has a brown information sign for Rushcliffe Country Park and the Transport Heritage Museum. Continue to the next roundabout and then turn right. The car park is on the left.

Nearest refreshments

Do I tell you about a small gem of a café? You will have to travel for another 4 miles along the A60 towards Loughborough. In Costock you will find **Six Acre Nurseries** and here there is the small **Garden Deli & Coffee Shop** which does wonderful sandwiches and great toasties. Would it help if I said they also have a very good selection of home-made cakes? The café is open from 10 am until 5 pm every day except Mondays (closed). They welcome dogs on leads, or food can be taken away. Postcode LE12 6XB. ☎ 01509 852339.

Dog factors

Distance: 4½ miles
Road walking: Two short sections on minor farm roads. There is a crossing of a preserved railway line.
Livestock: None
Stiles: None
Nearest vets: Ruddington Veterinary Clinic, Ruddington. ☎ 0115 921 2155.

The Walk

1 Walk past the country park buildings, keeping to the right. There is a lake in front of you. Dogs should be on the lead in this area. Turn right and take the wide path with the lake on your left. Take the next path on the left, still walking round the lake. Ignore the dog-walking areas on the right and continue to a T-junction.

2 At the T-junction turn right and follow the wider path to a Y-junction. Keep right here and follow the wide path with meadows on either side.

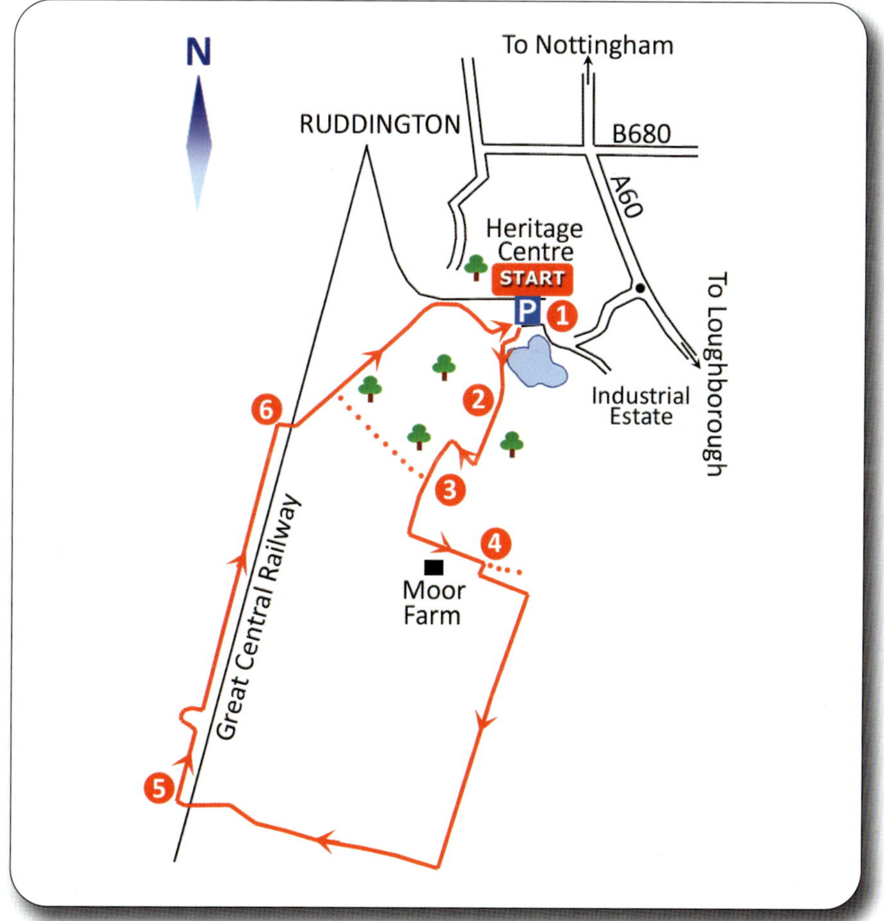

The meadows are home to over 100 species of wild flowers. There is also an abundance of birds in the park, including yellowhammer, reed bunting, dunnock and redstart. The barn owl boxes are also home to little owls and kestrels. Amongst the reptiles present are grass snakes, great crested and smooth newts, and red-eared terrapins.

Continue along the path passing a seat and a sign for The Hedgerows. Just after the sign take a grassy path on the left which bends to the left and reaches a yellow barrier.

3 Pass round the barrier and out of the park. Continue straight ahead up the tarmac road towards some farm buildings (**Moor Farm**). The road bends to the left with a farmhouse on the right. There is a gap in the hedge halfway down the road with a footpath sign.

4 Go through the gap and turn left. Follow the path round the field for about ¾ mile. Halfway down the field the path passes from the right to the left-hand side of the hedge. On reaching a T-junction, turn right and follow the path until you reach a railway embankment.

5 Cross the preserved railway line with care and directly turn right following a path with the railway line on your right for about a mile.

The railway line was part of the Great Central Railway which ran between Sheffield and London Marylebone. It was the last 'main line' to be built until the Channel Tunnel rail link in 2003. Due to its late construction, the company was able to take advantage of the latest technology, including steam excavators. The line was heavily engineered with viaducts and wide cuttings with a maximum gradient of 1:128; there were no sharp curves or level crossings which ensured a fast service for both passengers and freight. From the outset, the line had to compete with established north-south routes and it became the first main line to close in the Beeching era. The Great Central Railway PLC now operates throughout the year from their headquarters at Loughborough Central, running trains from the Heritage Centre at Ruddington as far as East Leake. The line north of Loughborough remained open for freight traffic to serve the gypsum mine at East Leake.

6 Eventually you reach a farm road. Turn right over the bridge and follow the road to reach a barrier. At the barrier turn right, back into **Rushcliffe Country**

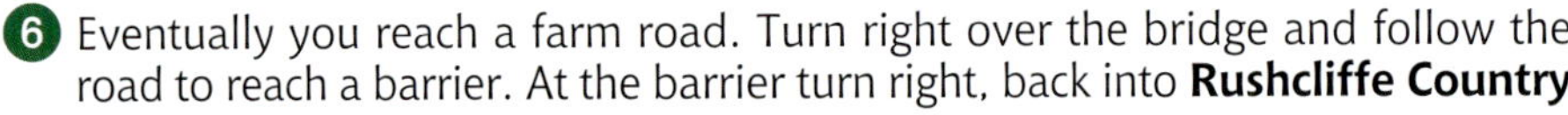

Park. Keep to the path on the left past the children's play area. It is possible to see the railway lines running into the Heritage Centre on the left. For a better view, stand on the white walkway bridge on the left.

The Nottingham Heritage Centre occupies the former Ruddington Factory Halt. No trace of the station remains, but the long building with the white roof is the original depot building. In the early 1990s a group of transport enthusiasts set up the Great Central Railway (Nottingham) Ltd, with the aim of re-instating the remaining line into Loughborough. The Heritage Centre is well worth a visit.

Continue along the original path which takes you back to the car park.

A photo call near the lake.

APPENDIX

The following are veterinary practices close to the walks featured in the book:

Buckley House Vets
51 West Street, Hucknall NG15 7BY ☎ 0115 9527 271

Buttercross Vet Centre
Long Acre, Bingham NG13 8AF ☎ 01949 837571

Candleby Veterinary Clinic
12 Candleby Lane, Cotgrave NG12 3JG ☎ 01159 893711

Lawrence Veterinary Centre Ltd
166 Nottingham Road, Eastwood NG16 3GG ☎ 01773 769298

McPherson Veterinary Clinic
166 Southwell Road East, Rainworth NG21 0EH ☎ 01623 798050

Minster Veterinary Centre
Malt Park (next to Homebase) Newark NG24 1HN ☎ 01636 612906

Minster Veterinary Clinic
Orchard Lodge, Newark Road, Southwell NG25 0EJ ☎ 01636 812133

Park Hall Veterinary Clinic
Park Hall Road, Mansfield Woodhouse NG19 8QX ☎ 01623 620784

Portland House Veterinary Group
53 Churchgate, Retford DN22 6PA ☎ 01777 703663; also at Rufford Avenue,
New Ollerton, Newark NG22 9PN ☎ 01623 860138

Raul Dowding, The Veterinary Centre
Narrow Lane, Bawtry, South Yorkshire DN10 6JQ ☎ 01302 711922

Ruddington Veterinary Clinic
2 Shaw Street, Ruddington NG11 6HF. ☎ 0115 921 2155

Thompsons Veterinary Surgery
105 Alfreton Road, Sutton-in-Ashfield NG17 1FJ ☎ 01623 555460

Vets4Pets
63–65 Wollaton Road, Beeston, Nottingham NG9 2NG ☎ 0115 9225 357

Wildbore Veterinary Ltd
5 Newcastle Avenue, Worksop S80 2AS ☎ 01909 472059